JERUS

Published by Gallery Books
A Division of W. H. Smith Publishers Inc.
112 Madison Avenue
New York, New York 10016

ISBN 0-8317-5208-4

Printed in Hong Kong

1 2 3 4 5 6 7 8 9 10

ALEM

PHOTOGRAPHY	MARCELLO BERTINETTI
TEXT	CARLO DE FABIANIS ROBIN LANGLEY SOMMER
DESIGN	MARCELLO BERTINETTI

GALLERY BOOKS
An imprint of W.H. Smith Publishers Inc.
112 Madison Avenue
New York, New York 10016
A Bison Book

This city in the midst of a desert has ultimately conquered all its invaders. Believers of every race and condition see in Jerusalem the pre-eminent Holy Place. Jews, Muslims and Christians live and worship here in sometimes uneasy proximity. The Old City, its walls reconstructed in the Middle Ages under Suleiman the Magnificent, is divided into quarters wherein custodians of the various shrines guard their precincts jealously. The divisiveness even among sects of the same faith, such as Latin and Eastern Rite Christians, exemplifies the conflict between universal ideals of brotherhood and the fragmentation of man's inner life projected into the world around him.

At dusk, when only the profile of the distant city can be distinguished against the backdrop of a crimson sky, the crosses crowning the Russian Orthodox Church of Mary Magdalene superimpose themselves upon the Islamic crescent surmounting the golden cupola of the Dome of the Rock, called by Europeans the Omar Mosque. Opposite the Wailing Wall, the only remnant of Herod's Temple, which was still under construction at the time of Christ, the Jewish Menorah shadows the warm stones, between which thousands of written prayers have been tucked. The sound of bells announces the Christian hour of Compline, while the chant of the *muezzin* calls the faithful to worship Allah, 'the forever existing, the One.'

Within the Old City are the Temple precincts sacred to Jews and to Christians as a hallowed scene of Christ's early life and public ministry. This 35-acre area also houses the splendid Dome of the Rock and El Aqsa Mosque, Islam's most important holy places after Mecca and Medina. Nearby are the Basilica of the Holy Sepulchre and the Way of the Cross taken by Christ from the Pretorium to Calvary, outside the original city walls (Jewish law forbade execution or burial within the city). Numerous other convents, shrines and monasteries commemorate epochal events in the histories of the three great monotheistic religions.

Modern Jerusalem has grown up outside the walls and is constantly expanding toward the Desert of Judea and the Dead Sea. Only by flying over the region does one realize how close are its ties to the desert and how much effort was required to make this forbidding site a major city. Its principal architects now are the men and women who created the modern State of Israel, many of them survivors of the Holocaust from every corner of Europe. Those who have settled here with the will to rebuild a long-lost homeland have faced a host of problems, not the least of which are the claim of Israel's indigenous Arab peoples and the hostility of adjacent Muslim countries. Generations have struggled to create both a national

Recent archaeological finds west of the Old City indicate that the walls of First Temple Jerusalem (seventh century BC) extended almost four times farther than most scholars had believed. Prior to this, archaeologists had debated whether ancient Jerusalem was truly 'the finest city not only of Judaea, but of the whole Levant,' as the Roman encyclopedist Pliny described it, or an obscure crossroad that was gradually mythologized into a splendid metropolis by its religious associations. 'Now we know,' says Gabriel Barkay of Tel Aviv University, in an interview with *The New York Times*, ' that it was a major city. This is critical also because a city that was the scene of the growth of monotheism and classical prophecy, a city said to be the only place you could worship God, had to have this importance reflected in its physical size.'

Today the majesty of Jerusalem the Golden, site of Solomon's Temple, can be experienced only imaginatively. Its physical remnants, called the City of David, comprise the Temple Mount and a narrow strip of ancient houses adjacent to it, now outside the Old City walls. The New City has long outgrown the confines of the ancient seven-gated walls to expand in all directions toward the Kedron Valley, on the east, and the Valley of Hinnom or Gehenna, on the south and southwest, which bounds Mount Sion. The New City, with its wider streets and attractive modern suburbs, owes much to European influence. The old flat-roofed houses and market stalls are surrounded now by modern buildings, wisely constructed in the same native stone for a harmonious blend of past and present.

During the day the fierce Mideastern sun beats down on the whiteness of Jerusalem in an effort to dispel every shadow and to penetrate even the gaps between the stones. The city appears to flatten itself in passive resistance to this assault: inevitably, the heat and blinding light will give way to sunset, when the glare will diminish to a rose-red glow pierced by the gleam of the sun's last rays on the golden Dome of the Rock. Then the dust raised by every breath of wind will take on the silvery reflections that promise respite in the shades of night. Wrapped in the cloak of its history, Jerusalem will subside into rest.

15 Jerusalem at dawn, with the walls of the Old City visible in the center of the photograph.

17 A bustling street scene at the Damascus Gate, on the north side of the Old City.

18-19 An aerial view of Jerusalem in which the medieval outlines of the Old City can be discerned, as well as the nearby Desert of Judea and the Dead Sea.

20-21 The cupola of the Basilica of the Holy Sepulchre, which covers the sites of Christ's crucifixion and burial, dominates the low houses and crowded streets of the Christian quarter.

22-23 Thousands of Jews are buried in this cemetery on the Mount of Olives, overlooking Jerusalem, traditional site of the resurrection of the dead at the end of time. Stones are a customary votive offering in the East.

24 Every year on Tu Bishvat, the Biblical Feast of Trees, collections are organized to plant additional greenery that will help win back more land from the desert.

25 Ancient olive trees in the Garden of Gethsemane, where the Passion of Christ began during the Passover Feast.

26-27 Mahane Yehuda, the Jewish market in the New City.

28-29 Arab commerce centers around the souks in the Old City.

30 The futuristic buildings of the Ramot quarter, designed by the architect Zvi Hecker, and of the city's new Jewish quarter, contrast vividly with the older buildings at the center of Jerusalem.

31 Modern buildings have also sprung up on the hills surrounding Jerusalem.

32-33 New satellite towns are reaching toward the Desert of Judea. This one, Ma' Ale' Adummim, is designed for an eventual 80,000 inhabitants.

34-35 The lights of the city at night add another dimension to the timeless mystery of the Damascus Gate, which opens on the road to Syria.

PEOPLE

Jerusalem's diversity mirrors that of the nation of Israel—a complex history of gatherings and dispersals, universal aspirations and deep divisions, material and spiritual advances alternating with violent upheavals, dissolution and slow reconstruction.

Dozens of languages are heard among these narrow streets, where multilingualism is the norm. This Tower of Babel effect is reinforced by the many styles of dress, from the uniform black of the Orthodox Jews to flowing Arab *baracans*, olive-drab military uniforms, colorfully embroidered Bedouin dresses and the austere cowls of Christian religious. Conservatives of all persuasions cast a cold eye on the vivid, sometimes scanty, dress of Western tourists with their ubiquitous cameras. Both Orthodox Jews and Muslims shun image-making as a form of idolatry.

Diverse habits and customs prevail even among segments of the Jewish majority, drawn to the historical Promised Land from all parts of the world. Some faces glimpsed in passing are seamed and weathered, as though carved by the ages. Others are fresh, eager, full of expectancy. All bear the imprint of the human quest for personal and collective identity, its focus sharpened here by decades of turmoil.

Although conflict is a commonplace, Jerusalem's people pursue their myriad ways with the tenacity of life itself. The city's parks and zoo draw children, lovers and those whose main occupation now is rest and reflection. Numerous cafes, tree-shaded squares and city gates are social centers for busy merchants, students and professionals. Housewives go out early in the morning to find the freshest produce in the markets and to share the small and great concerns of the neighborhood. Young sabra patrol the teeming streets with the confidence and energy of youth passing into maturity. Jerusalem is a vivid mosaic, a microcosm of the busy, beautiful, careless, diligent, acquisitive, sorrowful, ever-hopeful world.

37 A young Israeli mother caught in a moment of tenderness.

39 Bedouin from the surrounding countryside bring their flocks to market.

40-41 Typical Arab shops in the Old City.

42-45 The Arab community holds to its traditions in language, dress and customs.

46-47 The gradual onset of old age unites people of disparate ways of life.

48-49 Raising funds for new green areas around the city during the Biblical Feast of Trees.

50 A Greek Orthodox prelate takes part in the Procession of Palms, marking the beginning of Holy Week.

51 Strong family bonds have sustained the Jewish people through centuries of adversity.

52-53 Customers shop for the Sabbath at the Mahane Yehuda in the center of the New City.

54-56 Women are active and respected members of the Israeli Army.

57 A fellow sabra is mourned in the military cemetery, Mount Hertzl, on Memorial Day.

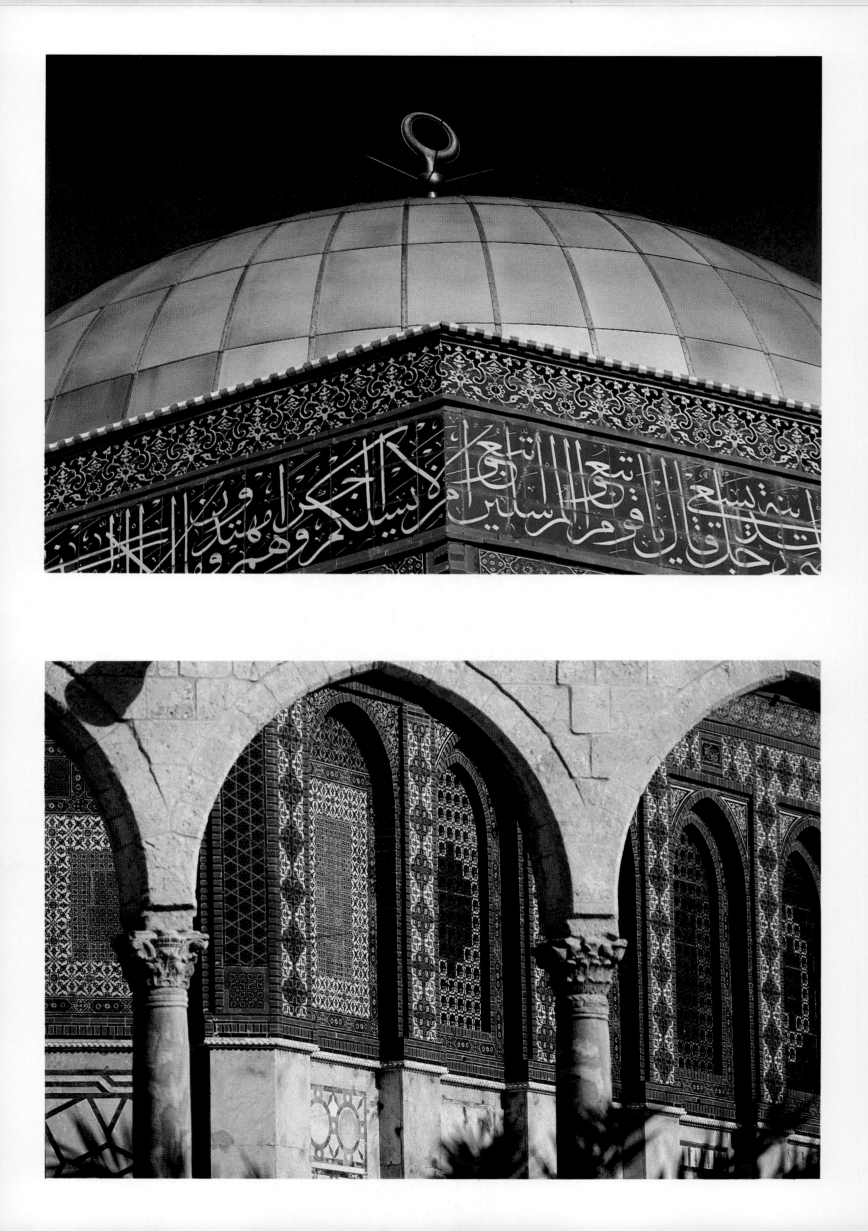

EC

חלמנו
CHELMNO

לובלין
NOWSKA

117
BERG

Jerusalem by night is unlike most modern cities of comparable importance: gaudy neon, glaring arc lights and hectic streams of traffic give way here to subdued street lighting, well-placed spotlights on important landmarks and sparse blinking lights in the New City. Peaceful dawns and sunsets, the natural rhythm of daylight and darkness, prevail.

The relatively small number of cars form tracks of light on the city streets, which are free of the usual urban pall of pollution. The ravages of time and technology are invisible here in the shadows of dusk. The Mideastern sunset comes abruptly, bathing the city in a harmonious glow of rose, gold and violet. The sun's last rays strike fire from the Dome of the Rock and signal the welcome coolness of the night. Street sounds that are confused and strident by day die off into the separate notes of a quieter theme, and Jerusalem seems suspended, an oasis in the surrounding desert.

Inside the Basilica of the Holy Sepulchre, the faces of lingering pilgrims are dimly lit by votive candles, as priests of the various congregations make their nightly rounds. The *muezzin* lifts his voice in the last of his five daily calls to prayer, and families regather in their homes for the night. Across the Kedron Valley, on the Mount of Olives, gnarled trees descended from those that sheltered Christ and his disciples stir in the evening breeze. When the sun finally plummets into darkness, only the seers can perceive the unbroken unity that lies here at the heart of the world. 'Behold, I have graven thee upon the palms of my hands; thy walls are continually before me.'

113   The night lights of Jerusalem are more subdued than those of most modern cities.

115   The full moon creates plays of light and shadow among the alleys, streets and cupolas of the Old City.

116-117   Sunset envelops the Old City and Mount Sion.

118-119   Spotlights illuminate the Tower of David.

120 The city skyline stands out against the lowering clouds of sunset.

121 Sunrise over the Holy City.

122 The newly renovated Jewish quarter of the Old City and the sophisticated Jerusalem Hilton are signs of Jerusalem's renewal.

123   The Russian domes of the Church of Mary Magdalene are an arresting presence in Jerusalem.

124-125   The minaret of El Aqsa stands opposite the Dome of the Rock on the Temple Mount.

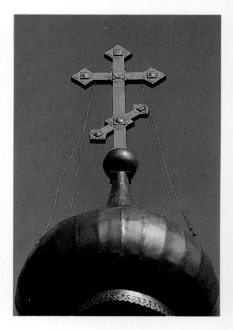

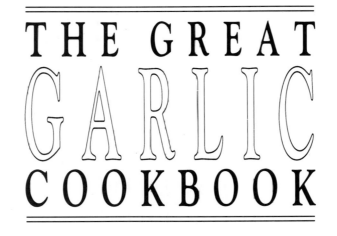

THE GREAT
GARLIC
COOKBOOK

SOPHIE HALE

CHARTWELL
BOOKS, INC.

A QUINTET BOOK

This edition published 1992 by
Chartwell Books
A Division of Book Sales, Inc.
110 Enterprise Avenue
Secaucus, New Jersey 07094

ISBN 1-55521-801-6

This book was designed and produced by
Quintet Publishing Limited
6 Blundell Street
London N7 9BH

Art Director: Peter Bridgewater
Editor: Polly Powell
Photographs: Trevor Wood, Michael Bull
Illustrator: Lorraine Harrison
Home economists: Felicity Jelliff,
Veronica Bull

Typeset in Great Britain by
Central Southern Typesetters,
Eastbourne
Manufactured in Hong Kong by
Regent Publishing Services Ltd
Printed in Hong Kong by
Leefung-Asco Printers Limited

Acknowledgement is due to Matthew
Hale for brotherly support; Marsha R.
Levine; Gail Harvey for the
prawnography; Tim Sisley for Arcadian
inspiration; Josephine Cruickshank;
Nick and Suzanne; and Beans for being
there.

The author and publishers wish to thank
the following for permission to reproduce
illustrations: p.6 Royal Horticultural
Society; p.7 ET Archive Ltd; pp 8–10
Casecross Ltd.

CONTENTS

INTRODUCTION

ARLIC has always been more than just a flavouring. In the course of its history it has been worshipped by the Greeks and the Egyptians, inspired the first recorded industrial strike, had binding oaths sworn upon it, been used as hard currency, to ward off the plague and the Evil Eye, to diagnose pregnancy and was reputed to cure anything from cancer to thinning hair. It has also served to preserve meat and corpses, temper steel, fortify in bed and on the battlefield, keep pests from crops and vampires from virgins, symbolize the union between man and the Cosmos; and has effectively divided the élite minority from the redolent masses across most of the civilized world.

GARLIC IN THE KITCHEN

ARLIC—*Allium sativum*—is without doubt the most versatile herb/spice/vegetable of all. Comparison with any other would be like setting a symphony orchestra against a penny whistle.

Often called the Stinking Rose, garlic is in fact a member of the lily family, and one of more than three hundred alliums, among which are onions, leeks, scallions, shallots, spring onions (green onions) and chives.

Garlic is, technically speaking, the strongest of these—"allium" is Latin for "odorous", and the Celtic "al" means "burning". But it needn't be. As the ultimate flavour of garlic depends on the way in which its sulphurous element—the source of its pungency—is released, the effect can be as crude, or as subtle, as you like. The quantities recommended in the recipes in this book, therefore, are not necessarily reflected in the strength of the final result: a chicken stuffed with 40 cloves of whole, blanched garlic and baked in a low oven will not be nearly as garlicky as a chicken served with an aïoli —raw garlic sauce—made with an eighth of that quantity.

Garlic can be rubbed around a salad bowl or fondue pan, or crushed or finely chopped and fried over a high heat to give a strong flavour to a sauce for pasta. It can be braised in butter as a delicate and unusual vegetable dish; combined with other herbs and spices for an Indian, Mexican, Mediterranean or Oriental flavour; and, used in sauces or marinades, it will give extra interest to bland meat or fish. Garlic is a marvellous flavour boost for canned soups, stews, *rechauffés* and cold cuts, and adds a certain *je ne sais quoi* to the *hautest* of *haute cuisine*. In fact, the only limit to garlic's range of uses is your own imagination.

As garlic can so easily dominate, it is not a good idea to have more than one strongly garlicky dish per meal. (For devotees, of course, anything goes.) It is also inadvisable to serve fine wine with garlicky food, as its subtleties will be lost. Robust reds such as Rioja or Chianti, or sharp dry whites like Frascati or Vinho Verde will all hold their own; cold lager is an especially good accompaniment to highly spiced or hot dishes; and Sangria, or a Spritzer—white wine with soda or sparkling mineral water and perhaps a sprig of mint—is also refreshing. Some people find that a strongly-flavoured sweet dessert wine such as Sauternes goes surprisingly well with curries. Garlic aficionados who make their own wine or lager might like to try adding a peeled clove or two when bottling.

When you buy garlic, make sure that the bulbs are firm and well filled out, and that there are no tears in the outer sheath. The skin of the bulb can be papery white, pink or purplish, depending on where it was

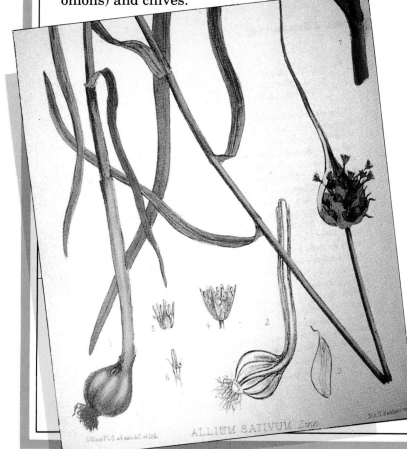

Left: The quantity of garlic in this 14th-century illumination gives an indication of how widely garlic was used medicinally, if not as an edible bulb, at this time

Opposite: A botanical print of *Allium sativum* from *Medicinal Plants* by Robert Bentley and and Henry Trimen, Vol. IV, 1880, drawn from specimens in Kew Gardens: 1 A whole plant; 2 Vertical section of the base of the stem and bulb: 3 Vertical section of the single bulbil; 4 A flower; 5 A flower with the perianth removed; 6 One of the inner stamens; 7 Blade and part of the sheath of a leaf

INTRODUCTION

Above left: Garlic chives growing
Above: In China garlic sprouts are eaten as often as the bulb itself

grown and at what time of year you buy it, but the flavour will vary little. If you want to keep it, store it in a cool, dry place.

A garlic press is handy if you use garlic a lot. Plastic is best. Bruise the clove lightly to loosen the skin, then crush it, unpeeled, collecting the juice and pulp as it comes through the holes. This makes cleaning the press a lot simpler; just pick out the skin and rinse the press under the hot tap.

As the smell of garlic tends to linger, it is a good idea to have a chopping board specifically for garlic and onions, and to wrap garlicky food in an airtight bag and greaseproof (waxed) paper, before refrigerating or freezing it. (Some people are afraid of smelling of garlic: parsley, chlorophyll preparations, absorbents such as peas and beans, and other breath fresheners will help—but why worry? Garlic smells like good food, whereas bad breath is bad breath.

GARLIC IN THE GARDEN

ALTHOUGH garlic can be bought all year round, it is easy to grow. It is hardy, but does need a period of heat and sun while maturing. To plant, carefully separate the cloves in a garlic bulb and put them—all except for the 2 or 3 centre ones—3½–5 cm/1½–2 in deep and 15 cm/6 in apart, pointed end up. If you are planting a lot of garlic, leave 30 cm/12 in between the rows. The soil should be fertile but fine and well-drained. Planted in early spring the garlic will be ready to harvest in autumn (fall) when the foliage has turned brown and started to shrivel. If planted in mid-autumn (mid-fall), it will be ready the following summer. Loosen the earth around each bulb with a fork and be careful not to tear open the sheaths when lifting them. Dry them off in the sun or an open shed, and shake off any loose soil. The garlic bulbs can then be strung together and stored in cool, dry conditions until needed.

Rocambole, also known as Spanish Garlic, is planted in spring—autumn (fall) too in very mild climates—3–5 cm/1–2 in deep, while Giant Garlic, also known as Elephant Garlic—much larger and more delicate in flavour than common garlic—can be grown in damper conditions and needs very little sun. The cloves should be planted 25–30 cm/10–12 in apart to allow for the size of the mature bulbs, and can be put in through to late spring.

Garlic can also be grown, an inch down in rich soil, in pots on a sunny windowsill; pots kept indoors near a heater should be well watered from the

INTRODUCTION

Above: This Indian woman is separating cloves of garlic, removing the loose outer skins using a large sieve

Above right: This chef with the flaming pan is cooking at the Gilroy Garlic Festival, an annual event held in Gilroy, California

bottom. (This also humidifies the room.)

You can grow garlic from seed, several varieties of which may be bought from seedsmen or garden nurseries. They will be able to advise you on what type to choose and how best to cultivate it, given the local soil and climate.

GARLIC IN FOLKLORE

ARLIC is probably best known, outside the kitchen, as a vampire repellant. In Bram Stoker's *Dracula,* vampire expert Van Helsing makes the Count's intended victim, Lucy, wear a wreath of garlic flowers, and rubs them around the window, door and fireplace as a first line of defence.

The Saxons of Transylvania—the very heart of vampire country—would stuff the mouths of suspect corpses with it before burial. A few cloves of garlic in the money bag were believed to keep witches from your gold, and, hung in dairies, to stop supernatural interference with milk production. If you gave garlic away, however, the "luck" would go with it.

Throughout antiquity, garlic was a protection for those most vulnerable to the Evil Eye: virgins, newborn infants (no Greek midwife would even attempt a delivery without a good supply of garlic to hand), engaged couples and the newly-wed. Indeed, anyone could be subject to malign influences at some time or another; and, if the worst should happen, and no garlic were to hand at a potentially hazardous moment, a loud cry of "Here's garlic in your eyes!" was believed to do the trick.

The Greeks used garlic to ward off the Nereids, jealous nymphs, invisible from the back, who would terrorize wives-to-be and pregnant women. It was also thought prudent to leave little piles of garlic cloves at crossroads to propitiate Hecate, Goddess of Destiny.

According to Homer, it was a type of wild garlic —moly—that prevented Odysseus from being turned into a pig by the enchantress Circe. So effective did this charm prove that she fell in love with him instead—further evidence for garlic's powers as an aphrodisiac.

Pliny, the great Roman naturalist, insisted that garlic juice would rob a magnet of its powers, while, more recently, strange rumours of the Garlic-Headed Tribe of Mexico swept the North American continent; and the Giant Garlic of the Southwest was responsible for more than one train wreck.

INTRODUCTION

GARLIC IN MEDICINE

CNE, alopecia, altitude sickness, animal bites, arteriosclerosis, asthma, athlete's foot, bee stings, bronchitis, bruises, cancer, catarrh, cold symptoms, constipation, eczema, epilepsy, exhaustion, flatulence, gangrene, greying hair, gastric disorders, headaches, hypertension, hypoglycemia, insanity, jaundice, leprosy, most poisons, obesity, open wounds, piles, poison ivy, rabies, scabies, sciatica, scurvy, senility, snakebite, toothache, tuberculosis, whooping cough and worms—these are just a few of the afflictions that garlic has been used to treat at some time or other during its long history.

The Egyptians, who were the first to practise medicine as we know it, featured many garlic-based cures in their pharmacopoeia. These were adapted by both Hippocrates, "the Father of Medicine"— who recognized its value as a diuretic and a laxative—and Discorides, whose medical texts were standard works until the late Middle Ages. (One of the latter's more endearing specifics was a combination of garlic, fig leaves and cumin to be used as a plaster on mouse bites.) Pliny, in his *Historia Naturalis,* lists no less than 61 garlic remedies. The Talmud recommends its application for tooth- and earache; the Chinese are believed to have used garlic medicinally since 2,000 BC; in India the five-thousand-year-old system of Ayurvedic medicine, featuring garlic-based cures for such ailments as heartburn, hoarseness and typhus, still flourishes.

During the Middle Ages, herbals—Thomas Culpepper's is probably the best-known—were both popular and widely available, particularly so after the invention of the printing press. Packed with plant-based remedies and lore—much of it to do with garlic—these books combined the folk medicine of the time (such as the tying of cut garlic cloves to the soles of the feet as a cough cure) and a growing knowledge of botany and natural science with the fundamental principles of what we know today as homeopathy, naturopathy and herbalism. They remained popular until the end of the 19th century, by which time the medical mainstream had turned to the more "scientific" methods of a newly-industrial society.

Although garlic was used in the trenches during the First World War as an antiseptic and antibiotic, and despite the strong support of the Soviet authorities—for whose people it was such a popular and accepted cure that it is sometimes known as "Russ-

Above: These two Chinese men are taking their morning exercise prior to visiting the Tong Reng Tan restaurant where meals are ordered according to physical state, not from a menu. All foods are herbal and many contain garlic.

ian Penicillin"—it is only over the last 30 years or so that garlic's medical applications have begun to be evaluated, or rather, re-evaluated.

Whether garlic is indeed that well-nigh universal panacea the ancients believed it to be, it is too early to tell, but evidence so far strongly suggests that it can control blood chloresterol levels, destroy many types of harmful bacteria, aid digestion, circulation and respiration and that it may be a possible anti-carcinogenic.

It is pleasingly ironic that such a technologically advanced country as Japan—currently in the forefront of garlic research—should be exploring territory covered 5,000 years ago.

GARLIC IN HISTORY

HE smell of garlic has permeated history for a good 6,000 years—longer, if you take the Mohammedan view that when a triumphant Satan quit the Garden of Eden, onions sprang from his right footprint and garlic from his left. (Staunch alliophiles, however, insist that garlic was the forbidden fruit that caused all the trouble in the first place.) There may be an unenlightened few who persist in regarding garlic as an aroma best confined to the Paris Métro or the occasional Mafia-owned fast food joint, but what other "flavouring" has meant so much to so many for so long?

Garlic is believed to have originated in the Siberian desert, been brought to Egypt via Asia Minor by

INTRODUCTION

nomadic tribes, and from there back up through India via the trade routes to eastern Asia, then westward to Europe. It was carried by Phoenician traders and Viking sailors to fortify them on their journeys and to treat any illness that struck on the voyage.

For all these cultures, whether Indian or Egyptian, Babylonian, Greek, Russian, Hebrew or Chinese, garlic was almost as important an element of their daily lives as salt. Had the Roman ruling classes been less snobbish about the pungence so beloved of their populace, one might now be receiving an "alliary", instead of a (salt-derived) salary. In ancient Egypt 15 lb would buy a slave; and, up until the middle of the 18th century, the Siberians paid their taxes in it: fifteen bulbs for a man, ten for a woman, five for each child.

For the Egyptians, the garlic bulb represented the Cosmos; its outer skins the various stages of heaven and hell, the arrangement of its cloves the solar system. Eating it, therefore, symbolized the union of man and universe, nourishing not only the body but the spirit. No wonder that the pyramid builders went on strike when their garlic ration was cut!

By the time of Horace, garlic was frowned on in upper class Roman households but consumed by the people in great quantities. Garlic was especially popular with the army, who planted it wherever they went, and it soon became a symbol of military life: any young man of a good family who wanted to enlist was told, *"Allia ne comedas,"*—don't eat the garlic.

A favourite garlic dish of that time was *moretum*, a blend of pounded garlic, herbs and the rind of a cheese. This sustaining and no doubt extremely pungent predecessor to aïoli was immortalized in Virgil's poem of the same name.

Marco Polo recorded the Chinese using garlic to preserve their raw meat and detoxify—and disguise the taste of—any that had gone off, while the Egyptians used it as part of the mummification process, and buried it with their dead. Six cloves of garlic were found in Tutankhamun's tomb, while painted clay models of garlic bulbs have been discovered in pre-pharaonic burial sites, put there to ward off any evil spirit that might impede the soul's journey to the afterlife. Bodies found in Theban tombs wear necklaces of garlic for much the same reason.

Garlic's protective powers against malign spirits, especially the Evil Eye, also applied to the living. In

FOUR THIEVES GARLIC

During the 1721 plague of Marseilles, it is said that an enterprising band of thieves became rich by robbing the corpses of its victims, protecting themselves from the infection around them by drinking wine in which crushed garlic had been macerated. This was subsequently known as *Vinaigre des Quatres Voleurs* and became a popular remedy for respiratory and intestinal disorders.

modern Egypt there is still a festival known as "sniffing the breezes" during which garlic is eaten, worn and smashed on doorframes and windowsills to keep malignant forces at bay.

Its efficacy at this was proved, to their own satisfaction, by the ancient Jews. If peeled or cut and left overnight a clove of it would turn black, a sure sign that it had absorbed all the "demons" from the surrounding air; and not just mystical "demons": medieval Jews would carry garlic in a pocket at times of plague, then throw away the "infected" talisman. They had acquired a taste for garlic, as well as the accompanying lore, during their sojourn in Egypt and the Bible tells us how they bemoaned the lack of it during their desert wanderings (Numbers XI) while the Talmud states enthusiastically that "it satisfies, warms the body, makes the face shine, increases the seminal fluid, and kills tape worms. Some add that it fosters love and drives away emnity . . . by the feeling of comfort it engenders." This passion for garlic earned them a Roman nickname, "the stinking ones"—one of the first excuses for anti-semitism?

Wherever it was popular, garlic was a class indicator, soon spurned by the upwardly mobile, the aristocracy and, in some cases, the clergy, but enthusiastically embraced as food and physic by the masses, causing the French author Raspail to dub it "the camphor of the poor". Such snobbery could prove fatal: during an epidemic in 1608, visiting French priests would comfort London's sick with no ill effects, due to the garlic they ate, while many of their English counterparts died.

In our own time, this Stinking Rose has become familiar in kitchens, gardens and medicine cupboards everywhere. No longer divisive, garlic is now the great catalyst, the creative spark that unites lovers of good food all over the world. This book is an appetizer. Dig in.

SOUPS & APPETIZERS

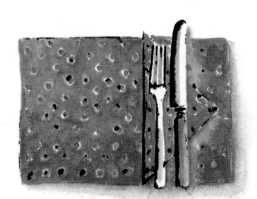

Opposite: Garlic Straws (*see* page 14)

GARLIC STRAWS

INGREDIENTS

MAKES 20

225 g/½ lb puff pastry

juice of 2–3 garlic cloves

¼ cup/50 ml/2 fl oz milk

5 g/1 tsp paprika

15 g/1 tbsp Parmesan cheese

salt and cayenne pepper

oven temperature
220°C/425°F/Gas 7

PREPARATION

♦ Roll out the puff pastry on a floured board into a rectangle, as thinly as possible.
♦ Stir the garlic juice into most of the milk and brush the pastry with half of it.
♦ Mix the paprika and Parmesan, and season with a little salt and cayenne. Sprinkle half of it over one half of the pastry.
♦ Fold the pastry and roll out as thinly as possible.
♦ Repeat with the remaining garlic milk and Parmesan mixture and roll out to a rectangle not more than ½ cm/¼ in thick. Brush with milk and cut into strips about 1 cm/½ in wide and 15 cm/6 in long.
♦ Arrange the straws, at least an inch apart, on greased baking sheets and bake for 7 to 10 minutes or until well-risen and golden brown.

————————TO SERVE————————

Serve warm, piled onto each other, log cabin style.

FRIED GARLIC HALOUMI

INGREDIENTS

MAKES ABOUT 16

1¼ cups/225 g/8 oz haloumi cheese, available from most Greek delicatessens

3–4 cloves of garlic, crushed

15 g/1 tbsp fresh mixed herbs, bruised and torn into small pieces

1¼ cups/275 ml/½ pint olive oil

PREPARATION

♦ Cut the cheese into 2½ cm/1 in cubes and pack them into a shallow soufflé dish in a single layer.
♦ Sprinkle over the crushed garlic and herbs, and pour over the oil to cover the cheese cubes.
♦ Cover the dish with a plate and leave in a cool place for at least 12 hours so that the flavours of the garlic and herbs permeate the cheese.
♦ To cook the haloumi, drain off the garlic oil and fry the cheese in a few tablespoonfuls of it until golden all over—about 6 minutes.

————————TO SERVE————————

Serve immediately with cocktail sticks.
Strained, the leftover oil is marvellous for salad dressings, marinades and frying.

————————VARIATION————————

To serve as a first course, cut the haloumi into ½ cm/¼ in slices, marinate, fry and serve with Sharp Gooseberry Sauce.

GARLIC BUTTERED NUTS

INGREDIENTS

1½ cups/225 g/8 oz shelled almonds, cashews or peanuts, or a mixture

2 tbsp/25 g/1 oz butter

15 ml/1 tbsp oil

2–3 cloves of garlic, finely crushed

rock salt

PREPARATION

♦ Loosen and remove the almond skins by pouring boiling water over them and refreshing in cold water. Rub the brown skins off the peanuts.

♦ Melt the butter and oil with the garlic in a heavy frying pan and toss the nuts in it over a moderate heat for 3 to 5 minutes or until they are crisp and golden.

♦ Drain on kitchen paper towels and sprinkle with rock salt. Serve warm.

VARIATION

For Devilled Garlic Nuts, add a little cayenne to the rock salt.

POTATO STREAMERS

INGREDIENTS

SERVES 4

2 large potatoes

2 cloves of garlic, sliced

¼ cup/100 g/4 oz butter

15 g/1 tbsp Parmesan cheese

salt and pepper

paprika

oven temperature
220°C/425°F/Gas 7

PREPARATION

◆ Peel the potatoes and cut into 2 cm/¾ in slices. Peel each slice round and round to form a long, thin ribbon.

◆ Soak the ribbons in iced water for at least an hour. Drain them and pat dry.

◆ Heat the garlic and butter gently in a frying pan until the garlic becomes transparent. Remove the garlic.

◆ Take the pan off the heat and dip each potato streamer into the hot, garlic butter and lay them on a baking tray.

◆ When all the streamers have been dipped, sprinkle the Parmesan over them and season with salt, pepper and a little paprika.

◆ Bake until crisp and well-browned which should take between 7 and 12 minutes.

◆ Serve warm.

-VARIATION-

Deep fry the dried streamers, drain on paper towels and sprinkle with garlic salt. Serve immediately.

CECILS, JAZZED

INGREDIENTS

SERVES 4—6

2 cups/450 g/1 lb minced (ground) beef
1 small onion, grated
1 cup/50 g/2 oz fresh white breadcrumbs
2–3 cloves of garlic, crushed
10 g/2 tsp tomato purée (paste)
5 g/1 tsp sugar
5 g/1 tsp paprika
2 dashes of Tabasco
15 g/1 tbsp mixed fresh herbs
1 egg, beaten
salt and pepper
½ cup/50 g/2 oz seasoned flour
4 tbsp/50 g/2 oz butter
30 ml/2 tbsp oil
1 cup/225 ml/8 fl oz thick yogurt
15 g/1 tbsp chives, chopped
15 g/1 tbsp parsley, chopped

PREPARATION

According to the Oxford English Dictionary, a "cecil" is a kind of meatball, and as for "jazz", here's Louis Armstrong's reply when asked for a definition: "Lady, if you gotta ask, you'll never know!"

♦ Combine the meat, onion, breadcrumbs, garlic, tomato purée (paste), sugar, paprika, Tabasco, herbs and egg, and season with salt and pepper.
♦ Mould (mold) the mixture into small balls about the size of a large marble, and roll in the seasoned flour.
♦ Fry them in the butter and oil for 5 to 10 minutes. Drain on kitchen paper towels and keep warm.
♦ To make the dip, mix together the yogurt, chives and parsley and season with salt and pepper.

————————TO SERVE————————
Serve the cecils with cocktail sticks and the yogurt dip.

MAMMY PATTIES

INGREDIENTS

MAKES 25—30

2 medium onions, finely chopped

22 ml/1½ tbsp oil

7 g/1½ tsp turmeric

5 g/1 tsp ground coriander

2½ g/½ tsp ground cumin

2½ g/½ tsp paprika

2½ g/½ tsp garam masala

Pinch of cayenne or chilli powder

3 cloves of garlic, crushed

1 cup/100 g/4 oz grated carrot

2½ g/½ tsp sugar

*¾ cup/350 g/12 oz minced
(ground) beef*

1 cup/175 g/6 oz cooked rice

salt and pepper

350 g/12 oz puff pastry

45 ml/3 tbsp milk

oven temperature
220°C/425°F/Gas 7

PREPARATION

A cocktail version of West Indian Patties.

♦ Cook the onions in hot oil with all the spices, except for half a tea-spoonful of turmeric, for several minutes, stirring well.

♦ Add the garlic, carrot and sugar, and cook on a lower heat for a further 10 minutes or until the onion is transparent.

♦ Add the minced beef and stir over a medium heat for about 7 minutes or until the meat has lost its pinkness.

♦ Stir in the cooked rice and season to taste. Leave to cool.

♦ Roll out the pastry thinly on a well-floured board. Stamp into 3 in/7½ cm rounds, using a glass or a cookie cutter.

♦ Form the trimmings into a ball, roll out again and repeat. Stack the rounds with a little flour between each, and store in the fridge.

♦ To fill the patties, pile a generous teaspoonful of the meat filling slightly to one side of the centre of each pastry round. Brush all round the rim with a little water and fold over the pastry to form a semi-circle. Press the wetted edges together with a fork and prick the top.

♦ Dissolve the remaining turmeric in a little hot water and the milk.

♦ Space the filled patties on well-greased baking sheets, brush them with the turmeric milk and bake until crisp and brown.

♦ Serve warm, and watch them disappear!

GARLIC TAPENADE

INGREDIENTS

SERVES 6

1 cup/100 g/4 oz black olives

2–3 cloves of garlic, coarsely chopped

⅓ cup/75 g/3 oz canned anchovies

15 g/1 tbsp capers

½ cup/100 ml/4 fl oz olive oil

a medium French loaf, thinly sliced

PREPARATION

♦ Stone and coarsely chop the olives and blend them with the garlic, anchovies and capers, adding the oil gradually.

♦ Toast the bread on one side. Spread the untoasted side thickly with the mixture and cook under a hot grill (broiler) until the edges are well browned. Serve warm.

♦ This can also be served on fingers of crisp, buttered toast.

CRUDITES

A selection of crisp, young vegetables served with a variety of dips is an attractive accompaniment to drinks before dinner, or as a supper dish in its own right. Allow 100–175 g/4–6 oz of vegetables for each person and ¼–⅓ cup/50–75 g/2–3 oz dip. Contrasts in colour, flavour and texture are important, so serve at least 3 different types of vegetable and 2 kinds of dip. Of course, the greater the number of people you are feeding, the greater the variety can be, but as some people do not like a strong garlic taste, have one mild dip like the yogurt and chive one served with Cecils, Jazzed (see page 17).

Suggested vegetables: carrots, courgettes (zucchini), celery and cucumbers, cut into narrow fingers; strips of red, green or yellow sweet pepper; cauliflower florets (flowerets); radishes; small spring onions or scallions; raw button mushrooms; cherry tomatoes. Cubes of melon or pear on cocktail sticks are also very good, especially with garlic mayonnaise.

Suggested dips: Aïoli (see page 55); Aïoli Verde (see page 55); Pesto (see page 54); Real Taramasalata (see page 30); Guacamole (see page 40); Ganoug Ganoug (see page 41); garlic mayonnaise—homemade or bought mayonnaise flavoured with Garlic Purée (see page 113) or garlic juice to taste; cream cheese softened with a little milk or single (light or cereal) cream and flavoured with a little crushed garlic, chives and parsley.

ARCADIAN GARLIC SOUP

INGREDIENTS

SERVES 4—6

15–20 cloves of garlic, unpeeled

75 ml/5 tbsp olive oil

5 cups/1 1/2 pt chicken or veal stock

10 g/2 tsp fresh thyme

2½ g/½ tsp salt

white pepper

3 egg yolks

TO SERVE

sliced French bread or toast

grated cheese

PREPARATION

In "The Passionate Shepherd To His Love", the poet Virgil mentions "a fragrant soup of pounded garlic and wild-thyme for the reapers wearied by the scorching heat". I like to think that this is the sort of thing he had in mind.

♦ Blanch the garlic for 1 minute, drain and peel. Cook it, but do not let it brown, in half the oil for 10 minutes. Add the stock, thyme, salt and plenty of white pepper. Simmer for 30 minutes and check the seasoning.
♦ Sieve or blend the soup, keeping a few garlic cloves whole. Return the soup to its saucepan and keep hot.
♦ Beat the egg yolks and gradually add the remaining oil. Stir a couple of spoonfuls of the soup into the egg mixture, remove the soup from the heat and add the egg in a thin stream, stirring well.

TO SERVE

Serve immediately with sliced French bread or toast, and a sprinkling of grated cheese in each bowl.

VARIATION

Omit the oil and egg yolk mixture and poach six fresh eggs in the simmering, unpuréed soup.

CREAM OF GARLIC AND MUSHROOM SOUP

INGREDIENTS

SERVES 3—4

2 heads of garlic (about 25 cloves)

4 cups/225 g/½ lb white button mushrooms, wiped and halved

6 tbsp/75 g/3 oz butter

5 g/1 tsp fresh thyme

4 tbsp/25 g/1 oz flour

⅔ cup/150 ml/½ pt chicken stock

⅔ cup/150 ml/½ pt milk

⅓ cup/75 ml/¼ pt single (light or cereal) cream

salt and pepper

TO SERVE

30 g/2 tbsp chopped parsley

50 g/2 oz button mushrooms, thinly sliced

PREPARATION

◆ Separate the garlic cloves and blanch them in boiling water for 1 minute, drain and peel.

◆ Sweat the mushrooms in the butter for 5 minutes. Lift out of the pan and keep to one side.

◆ Add the garlic and thyme to the butter and mushroom juices and gently cook with the lid on for about 10 to 15 minutes until the garlic cloves are just tender.

◆ Add the flour and cook for several minutes. Turn up the heat and add the stock and milk a little at a time, stirring well. Simmer for 10 minutes.

◆ Add the mushrooms and simmer for another minute to heat them through.

◆ Remove from the heat, stir in the cream and season with salt and pepper to taste.

————————————TO SERVE————————————

Serve sprinkled with the chopped parsley and thinly sliced crisp, raw mushrooms, for texture.

LEMON CHICKEN BROTH WITH HERB DUMPLINGS

INGREDIENTS

SERVES 6

2 cups/100 g/4 oz soft white breadcrumbs

1 clove of garlic, crushed

15 g/1 tbsp parsley, finely chopped

5 g/1 tsp dill, finely chopped

5 g/1 tsp mixed fresh herbs

salt and pepper

1 egg, beaten

a little seasoned flour

5 cups/1 1/2 pt well-flavoured chicken stock

juice of 2 large lemons

TO SERVE

6 sprigs of fresh dill

6 slices of lemon

PREPARATION

This delicate broth with herb-and-garlic-scented dumplings was inspired by the best Avgolemono *(Greek lemon and chicken soup) I have ever tasted, cooked by the substantial proprietress of a tiny family restaurant among the back streets of Rhodes.*

◆ Make the dumplings by mixing together the breadcrumbs, garlic, parsley, dill and mixed herbs. Season with a little salt and pepper, and add enough of the beaten egg to form a soft dough.

◆ Shape the mixture into small balls about the size of a large marble and roll in the seasoned flour.

◆ Bring the stock to the boil and poach the dumplings in it for 5 to 8 minutes.

◆ Remove from heat, add the lemon juice and adjust the seasoning.

————————————TO SERVE————————————

Add a sprig of dill and a slice of lemon to each bowl.

Opposite: Cream of Garlic and Mushroom Soup (*see above*)

FRAGRANT LETTUCE SOUP

INGREDIENTS

SERVES 4—6

6 cloves of garlic, unpeeled

2 large cabbage-type lettuces

45 g/3 tbsp onion, finely chopped

3 tbsp/35 g/1½ oz butter

4 tbsp/25 g/1 oz flour

2½ g/½ tsp sugar

salt and pepper

3¾ cups/825 ml/1½ pt milk or milk and water, mixed

2 egg yolks

45 ml/3 tbsp single (light or cereal) cream

TO SERVE

1 tbsp fresh parsley, chives or mint, chopped

Baked Garlic Croutons (see page 104)

PREPARATION

♦ Plunge unpeeled garlic cloves into boiling water and simmer for 8 minutes. Drain, peel and chop them coarsely.

♦ Wash the lettuce and shred it finely. Stew it gently with the onions in the butter for 5 minutes.

♦ Stir in the parboiled garlic and cook for a further 5 minutes.

♦ Remove from heat and add the flour, sugar and a little salt and pepper. Return to the heat and add the milk. Bring to the boil and simmer for 15 minutes, or until the vegetables are tender.

♦ Either sieve or blend the soup and return it to the saucepan. Check the seasoning.

♦ Combine the egg yolks and cream, stir them into the soup, and heat to just below boiling point (if boiled, the egg yolks will get stringy).

———————————TO SERVE———————————

Sprinkle the chopped fresh parsley, chives or mint over each bowlful and serve with Baked Garlic Croutons.

———————————VARIATION———————————

For a more intense flavour, add a handful of roughly chopped watercress leaves to the stewing lettuce.

FLOATING ISLAND SOUP

INGREDIENTS

SERVES 6

225 g/½ lb fish trimmings

1 good-sized bunch of parsley

2–3 sprigs of fresh dill

5 cups/1 l/2 pt water

1 medium onion, sliced

1¼ cups/275 ml/½ pt white wine,
or wine and water mixed

2 cloves of garlic, unpeeled

3 cups/350 g/¾ lb potatoes, peeled

1 small leek (white part only)

7½ g/½ tbsp tomato purée (paste)

2 egg whites

15 g/1 tbsp Parmesan cheese

5 ml/1 tsp garlic juice

salt and white pepper

TO SERVE

18 peeled shrimps

PREPARATION

◆ Simmer the fish trimmings, parsley, dill, water, onion and white wine with a little salt and pepper for 30 minutes.

◆ Cut the potatoes into 2 cm/1 in chunks, and the leeks into 1¼ cm/½ in slices.

◆ Strain off the fish stock into a clean pan and add to it the potatoes, the leek and the tomato purée. Simmer for 15 to 20 minutes, until the potato is cooked.

◆ Either sieve or blend the soup until smooth. Return to the saucepan and season with salt and pepper to taste. Bring slowly to the boil.

◆ Whip the egg whites with a good pinch of salt until really stiff. Fold in the Parmesan cheese, garlic juice and a little white pepper.

◆ Drop tablespoonfuls of the egg white mixture into the simmering soup and poach for about 5 minutes or until firm.

TO SERVE

Serve immediately with 3 shrimps in each bowl.

VARIATION

For a simpler soup, omit the egg white mixture and stir 15 ml/1 tbsp of single (light or cereal) cream into each bowlful of soup and serve with Baked Garlic Croutons (see page 32).

GAZPACHO

INGREDIENTS

SERVES 8

4 thick slices of white bread with crusts removed
60 ml/4 tbsp olive oil
15 ml/1 tbsp herb or red wine vinegar
4 cloves of garlic, chopped
5 g/1 tsp sugar
3 cups/1 kg/2 lb ripe tomatoes, skinned, seeded and chopped
2 sweet red peppers, seeded and chopped
1 medium onion, chopped
1 small cucumber, chopped
salt and pepper
iced water
ice cubes (optional)

PREPARATION

This is a summery cold soup, both filling and refreshing, and, depending on the garnish you choose, makes as much of a meal as you want.

♦ Crumble the bread and add the oil, vinegar, garlic and sugar. Mix in the tomatoes, peppers, onion and cucumber and either blend or sieve the mixture. The result should not be too smooth.

♦ Season with plenty of salt and pepper and dilute with iced water to the desired consistency.

♦ If it is a really hot day, add a few ice cubes to each soup bowl.

♦ Gazpacho can be garnished with any one or a combination of the following: sliced red and green peppers, finely diced cucumber, a dollop of Aïoli (see page 55), thick yogurt or mayonnaise; a swirl of soured (sour) cream; Baked Garlic Croutons (see page 32); stoned black olives; sliced hard-boiled (hard-cooked) eggs; sliced tomatoes; chopped spring onions or scallions; sliced sweet (Spanish) onion.

BOUILLABAISSE

INGREDIENTS

SERVES 8

1 kg/2½ lb fish
225 g/½ lb shellfish
60 ml/4 tbsp olive oil
1 large onion, coarsely chopped
4 cloves of garlic, crushed
2 cups/450 ml/¾ pt wine
15 g/1 tbsp fresh mixed herbs
a pinch of saffron threads (optional)
1 cup/350 g/¾ lb tomatoes, skinned, seeded and coarsely chopped
5 g/1 tsp sugar
salt and pepper
a little cayenne

TO SERVE

16 slices French bread fried in oil or Clarified Garlic Butter (see page 61)

PREPARATION

Variations on this substantial soup—almost a fish stew—abound all over the Mediterranean, the only constant being to use as many different types of fish as you can lay your hands on.

♦ Clean the fish and cut into equal-sized hunks. Small fish can be left whole. Scrub any mussels or clams and beard the mussels. Shell any prawns and, if using scallops, cut the meat out of the shell and halve.

♦ Separate the fish onto two plates, one for firm-fleshed fish and one for soft-fleshed varieties. Keep any squid or inkfish separate.

♦ Heat the oil in a large saucepan and fry the onion until it begins to brown. Add the garlic and cook for several minutes. Add the wine, mixed herbs and saffron.

♦ Simmer for 5 minutes, add any squid or inkfish and cook for 10 minutes. Add the firm-fleshed fish and cook for 10 more minutes. Add the soft-fleshed fish and simmer until almost cooked. You may need to add some water so that the liquid still covers the fish.

♦ Add the tomatoes, prepared shellfish and sugar, and season with salt, pepper and a little cayenne. Cook for a further five minutes, by which time any clams or mussels will have opened.

TO SERVE

Serve with the fried bread and a good dollop of Aïoli in each bowl.

STARTERS

Opposite: Real Taramasalata (*see* page 30)

REAL TARAMASALATA

INGREDIENTS

SERVES 4

50 g/2 oz slice of crustless white bread

225 g/½ lb fresh smoked cods' roe

2 cloves of garlic, crushed

90 ml/6 tbsp olive oil

lemon juice to taste

PREPARATION

The only thing this delicate creation has in common with the salty, pink, commercially-produced taramasalata is the name. This version is only worth making if you can get fresh smoked cods' roe, dark red and veined on the outside and reddish-pink inside. Cods' roe in tins or jars is always very salty.

◆ Soak the bread in water and squeeze out.
◆ Skin the roe and mash it together with the bread and garlic.
◆ Gradually stir in the olive oil, adding the lemon juice to taste.
◆ Serve with lemon wedges and Greek pitta (pita) bread, or as a topping for baked potatoes.

VARIATION

Taramasalata can also be made in a blender, although the texture will be much lighter and thicker, and you will need to thin the mixture with a little single (light or cereal) cream or extra lemon juice.

For Cods' Roe Spread, omit the bread and use half quantities of oil and garlic. Spread thinly on fingers of brown toast and serve with lemon wedges.

SORBET (SHERBET) TOMATOES

INGREDIENTS

SERVES 4

2 large beefsteak tomatoes

salt

2 cloves of garlic, crushed

freshly ground black pepper

a generous handful of fresh mint leaves

juice of 1 large lemon

10 g/2 tsp sugar

2 egg whites

TO SERVE

sprigs of mint

PREPARATION

◆ Halve the tomatoes horizontally, scoop out and reserve the seeds and cores.
◆ Sprinkle the insides of the tomato shells with a little salt and turn upside down to drain.
◆ Smear the inside of each tomato shell with the crushed garlic and sprinkle with plenty of pepper.
◆ Press the tomato seeds and cores through a sieve to extract the juice, and make up to ⅔ cup/150 ml/¼ pt with water.
◆ Combine the mint leaves, tomato juice, lemon juice and sugar in a blender. The mixture should not be too smooth.
◆ Pack into an ice-cube tray and freeze for about an hour, until crystalline but still slightly mushy.
◆ Whip the egg whites with a couple of pinches of salt until it forms soft peaks, and fold it into the semi-frozen mint mixture. Freeze until firm, stirring occasionally.

TO SERVE

Pile the sorbet (sherbet) into each tomato half and garnish with a sprig of mint.

SNAIL BUNS

INGREDIENTS

SERVES 4

4 large soft white rolls

3–4 cloves of garlic, crushed

½ cup/100 g/4 oz butter, softened

15 g/1 tbsp chopped spring onions or scallions (green part only)

15 g/1 tbsp parsley, chopped

salt and pepper

16 canned snails with shells

oven temperatures
220°C/425°F/Gas 7 and
180°C/350°F/Gas 4

PREPARATION

For many people, the high point of the snail-eating experience is mopping up the aromatic juices with fresh bread. Served this way, the juices are absorbed by the bread during cooking, which is then eaten as a bonne bouche. *The bun tops can be used for dipping.*

♦ Cut the top third off each roll and scoop out four depressions, each large enough to hold a snail shell.

♦ Mash the garlic with the softened butter, spring onions or scallions, and parsley, and season with a little salt and pepper.

♦ Drain the snails and put each into its shell. Fill the shells with the garlic and butter mixture.

♦ Put four stuffed snail shells into each bun, keeping them as upright as possible. Arrange them on a baking sheet and cook at the higher temperature for about 7 minutes or until the butter has melted and the snails are heated through.

♦ Cover with the bun tops and warm through at the lower temperature, while you seat your guests, and serve.

PRAWN (SHRIMP) PANCAKES

INGREDIENTS

SERVES 4—6

675 g/1½ lb cooked prawns (shrimp) in their shells

juice of ½ a lemon

one small onion, quartered

2 cloves of garlic, coarsely chopped

1¼ cups/275 ml/½ pt dry white wine

2½ g/½ tsp dill

½ a bayleaf

3–4 parsley stalks

a sprig of thyme

½ cup/90 g/3½ oz butter

1¼ cups/115 g/4½ oz flour

1¼ cups/275 ml/½ pt milk

½ cup/150 ml/¼ pt single (light or cereal) cream

salt and white pepper

PREPARATION

◆ Wash the prawns (shrimp) and peel them. Cover the prawn meat and put into the fridge. Simmer half the shells, the lemon juice, onion, garlic, wine and herbs in a large saucepan for 30 minutes.

◆ Make the pancake batter by sifting 1 cup/100 g/4 oz of the flour with a good pinch of salt, and stirring in the eggs. Melt 2 tbsp/25 g/1 oz of the butter and add to the flour together with enough milk to make a fairly thick batter. Leave to stand in the fridge for at least 1hour.

◆ Strain the prawn (shrimp) shell stock and reduce, if necessary, to about ⅔ cup/150 ml/¼ pt.

◆ Melt 2 tbsp/25 g/1 oz of butter and add the remaining flour. Stir over a moderate heat, without browning, for a couple of minutes. Add the stock and simmer for a further 5 minutes.

◆ Remove from heat and add the prawns (shrimps) and the cream. Adjust seasoning and keep warm.

◆ To cook the pancakes, stir the chilled batter well (you may need to add a little more milk). Fry one tablespoonful at a time in a buttered pan, keeping each pancake warm as it is cooked.

◆ When all the pancakes have been cooked, fill them with the prawn mixture and arrange in a buttered baking dish.

◆ Dot with the remaining butter and brown under a moderate grill (broiler) for 5 minutes to heat through.

◆ Serve immediately.

AVOCADOS WITH CAULIFLOWER AND BACON

INGREDIENTS

SERVES 4

2 ripe avocado pears (avocados)

½ cup/100 ml/4 oz good quality mayonnaise

7 g/½ tbsp Garlic Purée (see page 113) or 1 clove of garlic, finely crushed

⅔ cup/100 g/4 oz bacon, cut into 1¼ cm/½ in pieces

3 cups/225 g/8 oz raw cauliflower florets (flowerets)

PREPARATION

♦ Halve and stone the avocados. Widen and deepen the cavity a little by scraping out about 7 g/½ tbsp of flesh from each.

♦ Mash the scraped out avocado flesh with the mayonnaise and stir in the Garlic Purée or crushed garlic.

♦ Grill (broil) or fry the bacon until crisp.

♦ Mix the dressing with the cauliflower florets and most of the bacon and pile the mixture into the avocado halves.

♦ Crumble the remaining bacon and sprinkle over the top. Serve immediately or the cut avocado will turn brown.

—VARIATION—

Instead of mayonnaise, use ½ cup/100 ml/4 fl oz of Aïoli (see page 55) or Salsa Verde (see page 56), and omit the Garlic Purée or crushed garlic.

PAWPAW (PAPAYA) CRAB

INGREDIENTS

SERVES 4

2 ripe pawpaws (papayas),
275–350 g/10–12 oz each

¼ cup/25 g/1 oz whipped cream

½ cup/100 g/4 oz mayonnaise

Garlic Purée (see page 113) or
garlic juice to taste

lime or lemon juice

a little white pepper

1½ cups/350 g/¾ lb crabmeat

PREPARATION

According to Jamaican folklore, a goat tied to a pawpaw (papaya) tree won't be there in the morning. This luxurious combination of pawpaw and crabmeat will disappear a lot quicker.

♦ Split the pawpaws (papayas), and remove the seeds and "strings".
♦ Mix the whipped cream with the mayonnaise. As homemade mayonnaise is so much richer than a commercial brand, you may need to add a little more whipped cream to lighten it.
♦ Flavour to taste with Garlic Purée or garlic juice, lime or lemon juice, and a little white pepper. This dressing should be delicate.
♦ Combine the dressing with the crabmeat and pile into pawpaw halves.
♦ Serve chilled.

─────VARIATION─────

For Melon Crab, use two small melons, halved and deseeded, instead of the pawpaws (papayas). The fragrant, orange or peach fleshed varieties of melon, such as Charentais and Canteloup, are particularly good for this.

EGGS & PASTA

Opposite: Baked Eggs with Green Peas and Cream (*see* page 46)

BAKED EGGS WITH GREEN PEAS AND CREAM

INGREDIENTS

SERVES 4

2 cups/450 g/1 lb green peas, fresh
(shelled weight)

5 g/1 tsp sugar

sprigs of fresh mint

4 tbsp/50 g/2 oz butter

salt and pepper

8 eggs

1 clove of garlic, finely crushed

⅔ cup/150 ml/¼ pt single (light
or cereal) cream

oven temperature
200°C/400°F/Gas 6

PREPARATION

♦ Boil the peas with the sugar and mint for 10 to 15 minutes or until just tender.
♦ Drain, discarding the mint, and mash to a rough purée.
♦ Stir in the butter, and season with salt and pepper to taste.
♦ Divide the pea purée between 4 greased ramekin dishes and break 2 eggs over the top of each.
♦ Mix the garlic into the cream and pour over the eggs. Bake for 7 to 10 minutes, until the eggs are just set. Serve immediately.

VARIATION

"Mushy peas" are a woefully neglected vegetable, and this is a delicious and unusual way of serving them. Warm the contents of a 15 oz can, beat in a little butter, season with plenty of salt and pepper and proceed as for the green pea purée.

GARLIC PASTA

INGREDIENTS

SERVES 6

4½ cups/450 g/1 lb flour

2 eggs

15 ml/1 tbsp olive oil

juice of 2–3 cloves of garlic

30 g/2 tbsp well-drained spinach
purée or 15 g/1 tbsp tomato purée
(paste)

5 g/1 tsp salt

tepid water to mix

2 oz butter

Parmesan cheese

PREPARATION

♦ Mix together the flour, eggs, oil, garlic juice, spinach or tomato purée (paste), salt, and add enough tepid water to make a stiff dough.
♦ Knead on a well-floured surface for at least 10 minutes or until elastic.
♦ Divide the dough in half. Roll and stretch each piece repeatedly until as thin as possible. Leave for 15 minutes to firm up a little.
♦ Sprinkle each dough sheet with a little flour, roll up loosely and slice into ½ cm–1¼ cm/¼ in–½ in ribbons with a sharp knife.
♦ Boil in plenty of salted water for 3 to 6 minutes until just done, then drain and serve immediately with butter and Parmesan cheese, or whatever sauce you fancy.

SCARBOROUGH EGGS

INGREDIENTS

SERVES 2

3 tbsp/35 g/1½ oz butter

1 clove of garlic, crushed

15 g/½ tbsp parsley, chopped

2½ g/½ tsp fresh sage, chopped

2–3 blades of fresh rosemary, bruised

2½ g/½ tsp fresh thyme

salt and pepper

4 fresh eggs

PREPARATION

◆ Melt the butter over a low heat and add the garlic, herbs and seasoning. Cook gently for about 5 minutes until the garlic is transparent.
◆ Boil the eggs for 3½ to 4 minutes and shell them.
◆ Add the eggs to the herb and garlic butter and turn them for a minute. Remove the rosemary blades and serve immediately.

—TO SERVE—

This is the perfect dish for a light lunch. Accompany with plenty of crusty bread and a green salad.

PIPERADE

INGREDIENTS

SERVES 3—4

2 tbsp/25 g/1 oz butter

1 medium onion, thinly sliced

1—2 cloves of garlic, crushed

1 red pepper, seeded and thinly sliced

2 large tomatoes, skinned, seeded and coarsely chopped

4 eggs

salt and pepper

TO SERVE

a slice of hot buttered toast per person

15 g/1 tbsp parsley, chopped

PREPARATION

♦ Melt the butter in a heavy saucepan and cook the onions, garlic and pepper for 15 minutes. Add the tomato and cook for a further 5 minutes.
♦ Beat up the eggs with a little salt and pepper and pour into the vegetables.
♦ Turn down the heat and stir until the eggs are thick and creamy. Be careful not to overcook them.

———————————TO SERVE———————————

Spread on toast, sprinkled with parsley.

———————————VARIATION———————————

For a more substantial version, add 1 cup/175 g/6 oz of cubed cooked ham with the tomatoes.

GARLIC ROULADE

INGREDIENTS

SERVES 6

6 tbsp/75 g/3 oz butter

4 tbsp/25 g/1 oz flour

2½ g/½ tsp English mustard

1½ g/¼ tsp sugar

1¼ cups/275 ml/½ pt hot milk

30 g/2 tbsp Parmesan cheese

½ cup/50 g/2 oz cheddar or
gruyère cheese, grated

15 g/1 tbsp Garlic Purée (see page
113) or 2 cloves of garlic, crushed

salt and pepper to taste

4 eggs, separated

675 g/1½ lb fresh or 375 g/¾ lb
frozen spinach

30 ml/2 tbsp single cream

oven temperature
220°C/425°F/Gas 7

PREPARATION

♦ Melt 15 g/1 oz of butter in a saucepan with the flour, mustard and sugar, and stir for a couple of minutes, not letting it brown. Stir in the hot milk, a little at a time, and simmer for 5 minutes.

♦ Add the cheese, Garlic Purée or crushed garlic, and salt and pepper. Remove from the heat, stir in 3 egg yolks one at a time and keep warm.

♦ Boil the spinach in lots of salted water for 5 minutes, until almost tender. Drain and run cold water through it. Press out as much liquid as possible and chop finely. Turn into a pan with the remaining butter and a little seasoning, and cook gently for about 15 minutes to absorb all the butter. Check the seasoning and keep warm.

♦ If using frozen spinach, cut the block into small pieces, using a freezer knife. Melt the butter, add the spinach pieces and cook very gently until thawed, turn up the heat a little, cook for a further 5 minutes, season to taste and keep warm.

♦ Whip the egg whites with a pinch of salt until stiff. Beat a spoonful of egg white into the cheese sauce to loosen it.

♦ Carefully fold the cheese sauce into the remaining egg white and pour the mixture into a well-greased foil-lined Swiss roll tin (jelly roll pan). Bake in a preheated oven for 5 to 7 minutes until just set.

♦ Tip out immediately onto a dish cloth rung out in hot water. Spread with three-quarters of the hot spinach purée, into which you have beaten the remaining egg yolk. Roll up as you would a Swiss (jelly) roll—it helps if you gradually pull up one end of the dish cloth.

♦ Put the Roulade on a warmed dish. Stir the cream into the remaining spinach purée and pour round the Roulade. Serve immediately.

MASSAIA MIA

INGREDIENTS

SERVES 2–3

⅔ cup/100 g/4 oz prosciutto or cooked ham, diced

1 small clove of garlic, crushed

2 tbsp/25 g/1 oz butter

225 g/½ lb fresh pink or green tagliatelle

45 g/3 tbsp green peas, cooked

45 ml/3 tbsp single (light or cereal) cream

salt and freshly ground black pepper

TO SERVE

30 g/2 tbsp Parmesan cheese

15 g/1 tbsp parsley, chopped

PREPARATION

♦ Heat the diced prosciutto or ham and garlic gently in the butter. Add the tagliatelle to boiling salted water and cook for 3 to 5 minutes or until just tender.
♦ Drain the pasta and add the prosciutto or ham, garlic butter, peas and cream, and season with salt and pepper to taste.

TO SERVE

Sprinkle with Parmesan and parsley.

VARIATION

Heat the garlic in the butter and stir into the hot, drained pasta, together with ⅔ cup/100 g/4 oz of diced smoked salmon.

RAVIOLI

INGREDIENTS

SERVES 4

225 g/½ lb spinach purée

2 cloves of garlic, crushed

¾ cup/175 g/6 oz cream cheese or
low fat soft cheese

30 g/2 tbsp Parmesan cheese

1 small egg, well beaten

salt and pepper

½ quantity Garlic Pasta dough
(see page 46)

PREPARATION

As the amount of filling you put into each ravioli and the size you cut them out to can vary so much, the amounts given per ½ quantity of the Garlic Pasta recipe (see page 46) are only a guide.

♦ Combine the spinach purée, garlic, cheese and beaten egg. Season with salt and pepper to taste and leave on one side.

♦ On a floured surface, roll and stretch the pasta dough repeatedly until as thin as possible. Leave for 15 minutes to firm up a little.

♦ Brush half of the dough sheet with water and put teaspoonfuls of the filling on the wetted half, 2½–3¾ cm/1–1½ in apart.

♦ Fold over the other half of the dough and press down firmly round each little mound of filling.

♦ Cut between the ravioli with a sharp knife or pastry wheel to make squares of pasta with a mound of filling in each.

♦ Boil the ravioli in lots of salted water for 5 to 7 minutes or until the pasta is *al dente* and the filling heated through.

♦ Drain and toss with a little butter and serve immediately, with extra butter and Parmesan cheese, and perhaps a little cream.

VARIATION

To make an alternative filling, sauté ½ cup/100 g/4 oz bacon, cut into 1¼ cm/½ in pieces, with a clove of crushed garlic in 1 tbsp/15 g/½ oz of butter until the fat begins to run. Add ¾ cup/175 g/6 oz of chicken livers, 30g/2 tbsp of finely chopped spring onions or scallions, 5 g/1 tsp of finely chopped fresh marjoram and 2½ g/½ tsp of fresh thyme. Fry until the chicken livers are lightly cooked and the bacon crisp. Cool and pound or mash to a coarse purée. Season to taste with salt and pepper.

SAUCES & DRESSINGS

Opposite: Pesto (*see page 54*)

PESTO

INGREDIENTS

¾ cup/75 g/3 oz fresh basil leaves, finely chopped

30 g/2 tbsp pine kernels

½ cup/50 g/2 oz Parmesan cheese, finely grated, or half Parmesan and half sardo cheese

3 cloves of garlic, finely chopped

75 ml/6 tbsp olive oil

PREPARATION

Although Pesto is traditionally served as a sauce for pasta, it goes well with cold meats, grilled or broiled fish, in soups or on salads with a little extra oil and a dash of lemon juice. You can buy Pesto but if you can lay your hands on a plentiful supply of fresh basil it really is worth making your own.

♦ Combine the basil, pine kernels, cheese and garlic in a blender, and reduce to a thick, green, aromatic paste.
♦ Add the oil, a little at a time, until well incorporated.

———————VARIATION———————

For Walnut Pesto, replace half the olive oil with walnut oil and use chopped walnuts instead of the pine kernels.

AIOLI

INGREDIENTS

MAKES ABOUT 2 CUPS/500 ML/1 PINT

4–6 cloves of garlic (though of course you can use more)

a pinch of salt

3 egg yolks

2 cups/450 ml/16 fl oz olive oil

lemon juice to taste

a little water or single (light or cereal) cream (optional)

PREPARATION

Aïoli is simply the ultimate garlic sauce. Although originally served with prawns (shrimp), it is sensational on anything from hamburgers to Bouillabaisse, and a dollop of it will perk up the tiredest vegetable, rev up the blandest soup, and give yesterday's cold cuts a new interest in life. You can, of course, add crushed garlic or, nicer still, Garlic Purée (see page 113) to home-made or bought mayonnaise. It will taste much better than commercially-produced garlic mayonnaise, but it won't be Aïoli.

♦ Chop the garlic finely and pound in a mortar with the salt until smooth. Beat in the egg yolks.
♦ Add the oil, drop by drop at first, then in a thin stream once the mixture is glossy and beginning to thicken.
♦ Add lemon juice to taste, and if too solid for your liking, add a little water or single (light or cereal) cream.
♦ To stop a skin forming on the Aïoli, cover with a piece of plastic film that touches the surface.

———————VARIATIONS———————

For Almond Skordalia, add 15 g/1 tbsp of fresh white breadcrumbs, 15 g/1 tbsp of ground almonds, 15 g/1 tbsp of chopped parsley and a pinch of cayenne to each cup of Aïoli and flavour with lemon or lime juice to taste. This sauce is traditionally served with cold, cooked vegetables.

For Aïoli Verde, add to each cup of Aïoli a handful of parsley, two or three sprigs of fresh tarragon, two or three sprigs of fresh chervil and half a handful of spinach which have been simmered together in salted water until tender, drained and sieved or blended to a smooth purée.

Opposite: Aïoli (see above)

SALSA VERDE

INGREDIENTS

3 cloves of garlic, finely chopped

1 cup/100 g/4 oz parsley, finely chopped

15 g/1 tbsp watercress leaves, finely chopped (optional)

15 g/1 tbsp mixed fresh herbs, finely chopped (basil, marjoram, and a little thyme, sage, chervil and dill)

coarse salt

60 ml/4 tbsp olive oil

juice of 1–2 lemons

5–10 g/1–2 tsp sugar

black pepper

PREPARATION

Green and piquant, this sauce of fresh herbs is excellent with any fish, hot or cold, and goes well with hard-boiled (hard-cooked) eggs. Since it is so very good with prawns (shrimp), why not try it in a prawn cocktail?

♦ Blend or pound together in a mortar, the garlic, parsley, watercress, fresh mixed herbs and a little coarse salt, until they form a smooth paste.
♦ Add the oil, a spoonful at a time, and mix well. Add the lemon juice and season with sugar, salt and pepper to taste.

MARINARA SAUCE

INGREDIENTS

2 medium onions, thinly sliced
2 cloves of garlic, crushed
30 ml/2 tbsp olive oil
1½ cups/425 g/15 oz can of tomatoes
15 g/1 tbsp tomato purée (paste)
5 g/1 tsp sugar
5 g/1 tsp dried oregano
5 g/1 tsp paprika
salt and pepper

PREPARATION

♦ Fry the onions and garlic in the oil until they begin to brown. Lower the heat and cook for 15 to 20 minutes until soft.

♦ Add the tomatoes, tomato purée (paste), sugar, oregano and paprika. Cook rapidly for about 10 minutes until the tomatoes break down.

♦ Add salt and pepper to taste, and serve.

♦ This quantity of sauce is enough for 450 g/1 lb of pasta.

♦ Traditionally this sauce is served without cheese, but if you must, use a strong hard cheese such as Parmesan or pecorino.

—————————VARIATION—————————

Stir ⅓ cup/50 g/2 oz of stoned black olives and 30 g/2 tbsp of drained, finely chopped anchovy fillets to the finished sauce and heat through for a few moments before serving.

BASIC GARLIC DRESSING

INGREDIENTS

1–2 cloves of garlic, crushed

5 g/1 tsp sugar

30 ml/2 tbsp wine vinegar or Garlic Vinegar (see page 112)

75 ml/6 tbsp olive oil

salt and pepper

PREPARATION

♦ Combine all the ingredients in a screw-top jar, cover and shake well. Adjust seasoning before serving.

—VARIATIONS—

Include fresh or dried herbs to taste depending on what you are serving the dressing with.

Substitute different flavoured vinegars.

Substitute part or all of the oil with walnut oil.

Replace the oil with soured (sour) cream or yogurt and the vinegar with lemon juice (the cream version is excellent with 15 ml/1 tbsp of freshly grated horseradish added to it.

Add 10 g/1 tsp of mild French mustard. This dressing is especially good served over warm green beans as a first course.

CONCENTRATED TOMATO SAUCE

INGREDIENTS

2 medium onions, finely chopped

2–3 cloves of garlic, crushed

30 ml/2 tbsp olive oil

45 g/3 tbsp tomato purée (paste)

45 ml/3 tbsp wine or water

5 g/1 tsp dried oregano

5 g/1 tsp paprika

5 g/1 tsp sugar

salt and pepper

PREPARATION

This rich sauce can be served with pasta as it is, or with mince (ground meat) and liquid added. It is delicious poured over chicken pieces or fish steaks before baking, or used to top homemade pizza. It will also flavour soups and stews and is an excellent relish for cold meats, hamburgers and frankfurters.

♦ Fry the onions and garlic in the oil until they begin to brown. Turn down the heat and simmer, covered, for 10 to 15 minutes or until softened.

♦ Add the tomato purée (paste), wine or water, oregano, paprika and sugar, and season with salt and pepper to taste.

♦ Allow the sauce to bubble for 5 minutes, stirring constantly, and serve.

FRESH TOMATO SAUCE

INGREDIENTS

675 g/1½ lb ripe tomatoes

30 ml/2 tbsp olive oil

3 cloves of garlic, crushed

15 g/1 tbsp fresh basil or parsley, chopped

2½ g/½ tsp sugar

salt and freshly ground black pepper

PREPARATION

♦ Plunge the tomatoes into boiling water for a few seconds to loosen the skins. Run cold water over them and peel.

♦ Cut the tomatoes in half horizontally and gently squeeze out the seeds and juice. Chop them coarsely.

♦ Heat the oil and add to it the garlic, tomato pulp, basil or parsley and sugar.

♦ Stir over a high heat for 2 to 3 minutes until the tomato is heated through.

♦ Season with salt and pepper to taste and serve immediately.

GARLIC BUTTER

INGREDIENTS

½ cup/100 g/4 oz butter, softened

3–6 cloves of garlic, unpeeled

salt and pepper

PREPARATION

Garlic Butter is a great topping for steaks, hamburgers, grilled (broiled) fish or chicken and is a handy shortcut to Garlic Bread (see page 104). It can also be used to enrich soups, stews and sauces, and, in sandwiches, makes a welcome and tasty change from plain butter.

♦ Cream the butter until light and fluffy.
♦ Blanch the garlic in boiling water for 1 minute, drain and peel.
♦ Crush the garlic to a fine paste with a pinch of salt and gradually mix in the softened butter.
♦ Season with salt and pepper to taste, wrap in foil and chill until needed.

———————————VARIATIONS———————————

Parsley Garlic Butter add 25 g/1½ tbsp of chopped fresh parsley.
Herb and Garlic Butter add 25 g/1½ tbsp of chopped fresh mixed herbs.
Mustard Garlic Butter add 15 g/1 tbsp of mild French mustard.
Horseradish Garlic Butter add 15 g/1 tbsp of grated fresh horseradish.
Chilli Garlic Butter add chilli (chili) powder to taste, and 10 g/2 tsp of tomato purée (paste).
Tomato Garlic Butter add 15 g/1 tbsp of tomato purée (paste).

CLARIFIED GARLIC BUTTER

INGREDIENTS

3–6 cloves of garlic, unpeeled

½ cup/100 g/4 oz butter

salt and pepper

PREPARATION

This can be used for frying, especially potatoes, and can be brushed over pastry before baking, and over cooked buns and bagels before heating. It is also particularly good with vegetables such as asparagus and artichokes, however irreverent this may sound.

♦ Blanch the unpeeled garlic in boiling water for 1 minute, then drain and peel.
♦ Slice the garlic and heat gently in the butter with a little salt and pepper for 5 minutes.
♦ Skim the butter and strain it through a piece of muslin (cheese-cloth) or a very fine sieve. Keep covered in the fridge until needed.

FISH & SEAFOOD

Opposite: Slippered Salmon (*see* page 64)

GARLIC GRAVAD LAX

INGREDIENTS

SERVES 6—8

1 kg/2 lb middle cut salmon

4 cloves of garlic, crushed

⅓ cup/75 g/3 oz salt

⅓ cup/75 g/3 oz sugar

a handful of fresh dill, chopped

PREPARATION

♦ Split the salmon into two halves and remove the bone, but leave the skin on.

♦ Mix together the remaining ingredients.

♦ Place one half of the salmon, skin side down, on a large, flat serving dish and cover with half the mixture. Put the other half of the salmon over it and top with the remaining mixture.

♦ Weight down the salmon with a plate and leave in a cool place for at least 24 hours. Scrape off the mixture and serve the salmon cut into thin slices.

TO SERVE

A soured (sour) cream, mustard and horseradish dressing with a little fresh dill added is excellent with this dish.

VARIATION

Remove the bone, but do not halve the salmon. Cut into slices and spread with the marinade—see page 63.

SMOKED HADDOCK LASAGNE

INGREDIENTS

SERVES 6—8

12 cloves of garlic, unpeeled

675 g/1½ lb smoked haddock fillets

1¼ cups/275 ml/½ pt milk

a pinch of saffron threads (optional)

½ a bayleaf

1 medium onion, thinly sliced

4 tbsp/50 g/2 oz butter

4 tbsp/25 g/1 oz flour

15 g/1 tbsp Parmesan cheese

3 hard-boiled (hard-cooked) eggs

salt and pepper

350 g/¾ lb dry green lasagne

a little oil

1¼ cups/350 g/¾ lb ripe tomatoes, skinned and thinly sliced

5 g/1 tsp fresh basil, chopped

1½ cups/175 g/6 oz mozzarella cheese, thinly sliced

oven temperature
220°C/425°F/Gas 7

PREPARATION

♦ Plunge the unpeeled garlic cloves into boiling water and simmer for 20 to 25 minutes, until soft. Drain, peel and mash.

♦ Poach the fish in the milk with the saffron and the bayleaf for about 10 minutes or until the flesh is firm and flakes easily.

♦ Lift the fish carefully out of the milk, skin if necessary, and break into bite-sized pieces with a fork.

♦ Sweat the onion in the butter until transparent, taking care not to let it brown. Stir in the flour and cook for several minutes more.

♦ Add the milk – having discarded the bayleaf and any bits of fish skin – a little at a time and let the sauce simmer for 5 minutes.

♦ Remove from the heat and stir in the Parmesan cheese, mashed garlic, fish pieces, and the hard-boiled (hard-cooked) eggs cut into eighths. Season well with salt and pepper and leave, covered, in a cool place until needed.

♦ Boil the lasagne in batches in lots of salted water with a little oil to stop them sticking together. They should take between 10 and 20 minutes to cook until al dente.

♦ Lift each piece of cooked pasta out and run under cold water and lay on a damp dishcloth.

♦ When all the pieces of lasagne are cooked, use some of them to line the bottom and sides of a well-greased small, deep roasting pan or large pie dish (pie-plate) and spread over them half the fish mixture.

♦ Top with half of the tomatoes, sprinkled with half the basil. Add another layer of pasta, fish, tomatoes and basil, finishing up with a layer of pasta.

♦ Spread the sliced mozzarella over the top and bake for approximately 30 minutes until the top is crisped and well browned.

GARLIC MACKEREL WITH SHARP GOOSEBERRY SAUCE

INGREDIENTS

SERVES 4

2 large, fresh mackerel

2 small lemons

3 cloves of garlic, peeled

30 ml/2 tbsp oil

salt and pepper

2¼ cups/350 g/¾ lb sharp, green gooseberries

a little sugar (optional)

PREPARATION

◆ Wash and gut the mackerel, and cut three or four diagonal slashes down the side of each fish.

◆ Cut one of the lemons and one of the garlic cloves into four slices, and put two pieces of each inside each fish.

◆ Juice the remaining lemon, crush the rest of the garlic and combine with the oil, a little salt and plenty of black pepper, and pour over the fish.

◆ Leave the mackerel to marinate in a cool place for 2 to 4 hours.

◆ To make the sauce, top and tail (trim) the gooseberries and cook in a covered pan with a little water over a low heat until tender. Add sugar to taste and sieve the fruit.

◆ To cook the mackerel, drain off the marinade and grill (broil) under a moderate heat for 20 to 25 minutes, turning once and basting from time to time with the marinade.

———————TO SERVE———————

Accompany with the warm sauce and sweet potatoes.

SEAFARER'S STRUDEL

INGREDIENTS

SERVES 6

450 g/1 lb cod steaks

3 cups/350 g/¾ lb young carrots,
cut into 1 cm/½ in slices

2 tbsp/25 g/1 oz butter

15 g/1 tbsp parsley, chopped

⅓ cup/50 g/2 oz sultanas (white
raisins)

1 red or yellow pepper, seeded
and thinly sliced (optional)

1–2 cloves of garlic, crushed

15 ml/1 tbsp lemon juice

5 g/1 tsp garam masala

2½ g/½ tsp sugar

5 g/1 tsp turmeric

salt and pepper

2¼ cups/225 g/½ lb flour

1¼ g/¼ tsp salt

1 small egg

⅔ cup/150 ml/¼ pt tepid water

15 ml/1 tbsp oil

3 fl oz Clarified Garlic Butter
(see page 61), warmed

45 g/3 tbsp soft white
breadcrumbs

oven temperature
190°C/375°F/Gas 5

PREPARATION

*You can use bought strudel pastry or even filo pastry for this recipe, but
making your own is much more fun.*

♦ To make the filling, cook the cod steaks with a little water in a
covered pan for about 10 minutes or until the flesh is firm and flakes
easily. Drain and break into bite-sized pieces with a fork.

♦ Boil the carrots in plenty of lightly salted water for about 7 to 10
minutes or until tender. Drain, toss in the butter and parsley and
leave to cool.

♦ Soak the sultanas (white raisins) in hot water for about an hour
until they swell, drain and combine with the fish, carrots, peppers (to
give a bit of crunch), garlic, lemon juice, garam masala, sugar and
turmeric, and season with salt and pepper to taste. Cover and keep in
the fridge until needed.

♦ To make the strudel pastry, sieve the flour and salt together, and
beat together the egg, half the oil and most of the water. Stir into the
flour to make a soft dough, adding water if necessary.

♦ Turn the dough out onto a well-floured surface and knead with your
fingertips for at least 10 minutes or until elastic.

♦ Put the kneaded dough into a floured basin, covered with a cloth
and leave in a warm place for 15 minutes.

♦ On a well-floured surface, roll the pastry out as thinly as possible
and transfer it carefully to a large, well-floured cloth. Brush with the
remaining oil and leave it to rest for 15 minutes. Pulling gently from
the edges, stretch the dough until it is paper thin.

♦ Cut off the thickened edges and brush the dough with two thirds of
the Clarified Garlic Butter.

♦ Sprinkle over the breadcrumbs, and lay the filling down one edge of
the dough, leaving a couple of inches free at either end. Fold over and
roll up the strudel.

♦ Slide it onto a well-greased baking sheet—you may need to bend the
strudel into a horseshoe to get it on—and brush thoroughly with the
remaining Clarified Garlic Butter.

♦ Bake for about 30 minutes and serve, cut into thick, slanting slices.

QUENELLES WITH PINK FENNEL SAUCE

INGREDIENTS

SERVES 4—6

675 g/1½ lb white fish fillets

2 cloves of garlic, finely crushed

1¼ cups/275 ml/½ pt water

2½ g/½ tsp salt

½ cup/100 g/4 oz butter

1 cup/100 g/4 oz flour, sieved

2 eggs, and 2 egg whites

salt and pepper

30 ml/2 tbsp chilled single (light or cereal) cream

fish stock or water

1 × 225 g/8 oz head fennel

15 g/1 tbsp onion, finely chopped

30 ml/2 tbsp white wine

¾ cup/225 g/½ lb tomatoes, skinned, seeded and chopped

2½ g/½ tsp sugar

350 g/¾ lb green tagliatelle or fettucine

7½ g/1½ tsp fennel seeds

PREPARATION

This may be fiddly to prepare but the result is certainly worth the effort.

♦ Blend the fish to a smooth purée with the garlic and refrigerate.

♦ Bring the water, the salt and half the butter to the boil. When the butter has melted, remove from the heat and tip in the flour.

♦ Beat over a moderate heat until the mixture leaves the sides of the pan and forms a mass.

♦ Remove from the heat and beat in the eggs and the extra whites, one at a time. Turn into a mixing bowl and add the raw fish and garlic purée. Beat in the cream and season with salt and pepper to taste.

♦ Form into 16 quenelles using two wetted dessertspoons by filling one spoon with the mixture and using the other to round the top.

♦ Poach the quenelles as soon as all have been shaped, in a deep frying pan of barely simmering fish stock or water for 15 to 20 minutes. Lift them out, cover with a piece of greased foil and keep warm.

♦ To make the sauce, chop the fennel finely, and sweat it with the onion, wine and half the remaining butter until tender.

♦ Mix in the chopped tomatoes and sugar and blend to a smooth purée. Season with salt and pepper to taste and keep warm.

♦ Cook the pasta in lightly salted boiling water until *al dente*, drain, toss in the remaining butter and the fennel seeds, and put in a heated serving dish.

♦ Arrange the warm quenelles on the pasta, pour on the sauce and serve.

—VARIATION—

The quenelle mixture can also be served as individual fish mousses. Pack into well-buttered individual soufflé dishes or ramekins, set them in a roasting pan half-full of boiling water and bake at 180°C/350°F/Gas 4 until the mousses have risen and drawn away from the sides of their dishes.

Jamaican Grilled Lobster

INGREDIENTS

SERVES 4

2 cooked lobsters (best when heavy
for their size), weighing about
675 g/1½ lb each

a little oil

6 tbsp/75 g/3 oz butter

2 cloves of garlic, finely crushed

10 g/2 tsp mixed fresh herbs or
5 g/1 tsp dried mixed herbs

2 pinches cayenne

30 g/2 tbsp finely chopped spring
onions or scallions (green part only)

30 g/2 tbsp chopped parsley

45 g/3 tbsp fresh white breadcrumbs

salt and pepper

PREPARATION

♦ Split each lobster in half, leaving the head and small claws on. Remove the meat from the head and tail and discard the intestine, stomach and gills. Crack the claws carefully and extract the meat.

♦ Cut the lobster meat into bite-sized pieces and brush the outsides of the shells with a little oil, to keep them shiny.

♦ Shortly before serving, melt 4 tbsp/50 g/2 oz of the butter over a low heat with the garlic and add the lobster meat, mixed herbs, cayenne, spring onions or scallions, and a little salt and pepper.

♦ Heat the meat through gently, for 2 to 3 minutes, shaking the pan from time to time. Pile back into the shells and top with the parsley and breadcrumbs.

♦ Dot with the remaining butter and cook under a hot, preheated grill (broiler) for 5 to 7 minutes, until the topping is crisp and golden.

---TO SERVE---

Serve immediately, accompanied by rum punch, lager or beer.

Honey Garlic Prawns (Shrimp)

INGREDIENTS

SERVES 4

675 g/1½ lb large, raw prawns
(shrimp)

3 cloves of garlic, crushed

juice of 2 lemons

10 g/2 tsp sugar

15 ml/1 tbsp soy sauce

30 ml/2 tbsp olive oil

freshly ground black pepper

1 cup/100 g/4 oz flour

2 pinches salt

1 egg

⅔ cup/150 ml/¼ pint milk and
water

30 ml/2 tbsp honey

2½ cm/1 in root ginger, grated

10 g/2 tsp cornflour (cornstarch)

15 g/1 tbsp sesame seeds

PREPARATION

♦ Peel the prawns (shrimp) and cut deeply along the back of each, removing the main vein.

♦ Combine the crushed garlic, lemon juice, sugar, soy sauce, half the oil and a good shake of black pepper. Pour over the prawns and leave to marinate in a cool place for 2 to 4 hours.

♦ Make the batter by sifting together the flour and salt. Add the egg, the remaining oil and finally the milk and water mixture, a little at a time, until the batter will coat the back of a spoon. Store in the fridge.

♦ Drain the prawns and reserve the marinade. Dip each prawn in the batter and deep fry for 1½ minutes in very hot fat until crisp and golden.

♦ Drain the prawns on kitchen paper towels and keep warm in a serving dish.

♦ Heat the remaining marinade with the honey, grated ginger and cornflour. Stir constantly until the sauce thickens. Allow to simmer, still stirring, for several minutes.

♦ Pour the sauce over the prawns and turn them gently in it until well coated. Sprinkle with the sesame seeds and serve immediately.

MEAT & POULTRY

Opposite: Saltimbocca (*see* page 74)

SALTIMBOCCA

INGREDIENTS

SERVES 4

8 thin slices veal, about 7½ ×
10 cm/3 × 4 in

8 thin slices cooked ham or
prosciutto,
about 7½ × 10 cm/3 × 4 in

8 thin slices mozzarella cheese

fresh or dried sage

30 ml/2 tbsp olive oil

2 cloves of garlic, crushed

juice of 1 large lemon

salt and pepper

4 tbsp/50 g/2 oz butter

½ cup/100 ml/4 fl oz white wine

15 g/1 tbsp finely chopped spring
onions or scallions (green part only)

TO SERVE

15 g/1 tbsp parsley, chopped

sprigs of parsley

lemon wedges

PREPARATION

♦ On each slice of veal lay a slice of ham, a slice of cheese and either a quarter of a well-bruised leaf of fresh sage or a tiny pinch of dried sage. Roll up and secure with a cocktail stick.
♦ Mix the olive oil, garlic, and half the lemon juice, and season with salt, pepper and a little fresh or dried sage.
♦ Pour over the veal rolls and leave in a cool place to marinate for 2 to 4 hours.
♦ To cook, heat the butter in a large frying pan and gently sauté the veal rolls for about 10 minutes, turning occasionally.
♦ Turn up the heat and add the wine, chopped spring onions or scallions, and the remaining lemon juice.
♦ Allow the sauce to bubble and reduce for 5 minutes. Check the seasoning.

TO SERVE

Sprinkle with the parsley and serve immediately, garnished with parsley sprigs and lemon wedges.

BEEF NAPOLEON

INGREDIENTS

SERVES 6

2 heads garlic

45 ml/3 tbsp olive oil

60 ml/4 tbsp robust red wine

30 g/2 tbsp finely chopped spring
onions or scallions

7½ g/2½ tsp fresh thyme or
2½ g/1½ tsp dried thyme

15 g/3 tsp French mustard

salt and pepper

1 beef fillet, weighing about
1 kg/2 lb

30 g/2 tbsp chopped parsley

450 g/1 lb puff pastry

oven temperature
230°C/450°F/Gas 8

PREPARATION

As Beef Wellington is getting somewhat overexposed, considering that it was inspired by a man best known for his contribution to his nation's footwear, here is a suitably historical alternative.

♦ To prepare the marinade, peel and crush 3 of the garlic cloves and mix with 30 ml/2 tbsp of the oil, the wine, spring onions or scallions, 15 g/1 tsp of the mustard, the thyme, and plenty of salt and pepper.
♦ Lay the fillet at the bottom of a large plastic bag and pour the marinade in over it. Seal the top of the bag, put it on a plate in case of leaks, and leave to marinate in a cool place for 6–8 hours.
♦ Heat the remaining oil in a large frying pan until very hot.
♦ Lift the meat out of its marinade and fry it quickly on all sides to seal in the juices; this should take no more than 2 minutes.
♦ Cool the beef and return to its marinade. Freeze for an hour—more if you like your fillet really rare.
♦ Simmer the remaining unpeeled garlic cloves for 20 to 25 minutes, until soft. Drain, peel and mash with a fork to a sticky paste.
♦ Stir in the remaining mustard and the parsley, and season with salt and pepper to taste.
♦ Take the beef out of the freezer and leave, to thaw the marinade. Roll out the pastry to a thickness of ½ cm/¼ in—large enough to wrap the beef generously.

BEEF NAPOLEON

♦ Drain the meat and add a tablespoonful of its marinade to the garlic and parsley mixture.

♦ Lay the beef in the middle of the pastry and spread the garlic and parsley mixture over it.

♦ Wet the edges of the pastry with a little water, bring them up over the sides of the meat, and press them together. Seal the ends.

♦ Put the pastry-wrapped beef, seam side down, on a well greased baking tray (sheet), brush the top with a little milk or egg yolk, and bake for 15 to 20 minutes, until the pastry is cooked. If, after this time, the pastry is cooked but the fillet is too rare turn down the heat to 190°C/375°F/Gas 5 and cook for a further 7 to 10 minutes, and test again. Serve immediately.

———————————————VARIATION———————————————

For Beef Garibaldi, spread the beef with half a cup of Pesto (see page 54) instead of the garlic and parsley paste.

COTTABULLA

INGREDIENTS

SERVES 8

225 g/½ lb stale white bread, crusts removed

1 kg/2 lb minced (ground) beef

2 medium onions, finely chopped

2 eggs

5 g/1 tsp ground coriander

5 g/1 tsp dried oregano

15 g/1 tbsp paprika

3 cloves of garlic, crushed

a pinch of cayenne

5 g/1 tsp sugar

salt and freshly ground black pepper

oven temperature
190°C/375°F/Gas 5

PREPARATION

The origins of this old family recipe are obscured in a West Indian mist, but there is nothing vague about Cottabulla itself—a tasty cross between a cold meatloaf and a pâté campagne.

♦ Soak the bread in water, squeeze out and crumble. Mix all the ingredients together thoroughly, seasoning with plenty of salt and pepper.
♦ Pack into a large soufflé dish leaving a slight hollow in the middle. Cover with foil and bake for 40 to 50 minutes until cooked through, but still slightly pink in the middle.
♦ While it is still hot, put a plate slightly smaller than the baking dish on top of the foil and weight it with some heavy cans. Leave until cold and firm, remove the weights and refrigerate until needed.

——————TO SERVE——————

Slice into wedges and serve in its cooking dish.

——————VARIATION——————

This can also be served hot—see the illustration—there is no need to weight it.

Shaped into patties, rolled in seasoned flour and fried, grilled or barbecued, this mixture makes sensational hamburgers!

BEEF COBBLER

INGREDIENTS

SERVES 6—8

1 kg/2 lb stewing steak
1/2 cup/50 g/2 oz seasoned flour
60 ml/4 tbsp oil
4 cups/450 g/1 lb onions, cut into 2 1/2 cm/1 in chunks
4—5 cloves of garlic, crushed
3 cups/350 g/3/4 lb large carrots, cut into 1 cm/1/2 in rounds
10 g/2 tsp dried mixed herbs
5 g/1 tsp sugar
15 g/1 tbsp paprika
15 ml/1 tbsp tomato purée (paste)
1 1/4 cups/275 ml/1/2 pt red wine
1 1/4 cups/275 ml/1/2 pt stock or water
salt and pepper
2 1/4 cups/225 g/8 oz plain (all-purpose) flour
12 1/2 g/2 1/2 tsp baking powder
4 tbsp/50 g/2 oz butter or shortening
2/3 cup/150 ml/1/4 pt cold milk & water

oven temperatures
200°C/400°F/Gas 6 and
160°C/325°F/Gas 3

PREPARATION

♦ Trim the meat of fat and membrane and cut into 3 cm/1 1/4 in chunks. Roll in the seasoned flour and fry rapidly in the oil in batches until browned all over. Transfer the meat to a large casserole and sprinkle with any remaining seasoned flour.

♦ Fry the onions and garlic until they begin to brown and add to the casserole together with the carrots, herbs, sugar, paprika, tomato purée, wine, stock or water, and plenty of salt and pepper.

♦ Stir gently and put the uncovered casserole into a hot oven for 20 minutes. Stir after 10 minutes.

♦ Cover the casserole with foil, put its lid on and cook at the lower temperature for a further 2 hours, stirring from time to time. Add more stock or water if it looks dry.

♦ To make the scone topping, sift the flour and baking powder together and rub in the butter or shortening until the mixture resembles fine breadcrumbs.

♦ Add plenty of salt and pepper and enough milk and water to make a soft dough.

♦ Roll out to a 1 cm/1/2 in thickness on a well-floured surface and stamp out circles 3 1/2—5 cm/1 1/2—2 in across.

♦ Taste the stew and adjust the seasoning, adding a little more stock or water if necessary.

♦ Arrange the scone circles on top of the hot stew and cook, uncovered, at the higher temperature for 20 to 30 minutes, until the scones are puffy and well browned.

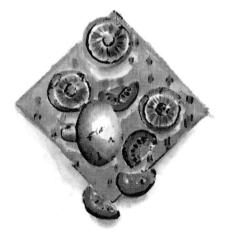

PASTA AL PASTORE

INGREDIENTS

SERVES 6

675 g/1½ lb potatoes

2 medium onions, finely chopped

2 cloves of garlic, crushed

45 ml/3 tbsp olive oil

30 g/2 tbsp tomato purée (paste)

⅔ cup/175 ml/¼ pt red wine

5 g/1 tsp oregano, or 10 g/2 tsp
fresh marjoram, chopped

5 g/1 tsp dried basil, or 10 g/2 tsp
finely chopped fresh basil

10 g/2 tsp paprika   5 g/1 tsp sugar

salt and pepper

3 cups/675 g/1½ lb minced
(ground) beef

4 tbsp/50 g/2 oz butter

30 ml/2 tbsp single (light cereal) cream

15 g/1 tbsp Parmesan cheese, or
30 g/2 tbsp grated cheddar cheese

oven temperature
200°C/400°F/Gas 6

PREPARATION

◆ Peel the potatoes and cut into 2½ cm/1 in chunks. Boil them in plenty of salted water for about 15 minutes, until tender.

◆ Meanwhile, soften the onions and garlic in the olive oil over a low heat, then turn up the heat and add the tomato purée, wine, herbs, paprika and sugar and season with salt and pepper.

◆ Add the beef and cook over a moderate heat for about 10 minutes, stirring from time to time, until the meat loses its pinkness.

◆ Drain the potatoes, season with plenty of salt and pepper and mash well, adding first the butter and then the cream.

◆ Spread the warm beef in a baking dish and cover with the mashed potato.

◆ Sprinkle with the cheese and bake for 20 to 30 minutes, depending on the thickness of the meat and potato.

◆ Brown the top under a hot grill (broiler).

RACK OF LAMB IN A GARLIC CRUST

INGREDIENTS

SERVES 4—6

*2 racks of lamb of 6—8 chops
each, chined*

3 cloves of garlic, peeled

a sprig of rosemary

15 ml/1 tbsp oil

*45 g/3 tbsp fresh white
breadcrumbs*

*30 g/2 tbsp redcurrant or guava
jelly, warmed*

15 g/1 tbsp parsley, chopped

2½ g/½ tsp French mustard

salt and pepper

oven temperature
230°C/450°F/Gas 8

PREPARATION

◆ Turn the lamb racks bone side up and cut a narrow slit between each chop at the meaty end.
◆ Slice one clove of garlic and stuff each slit with a sliver of garlic and a blade of rosemary.
◆ Put the lamb racks, fat side up, into an oiled roasting pan and cut several shallow diagonal slashes in the fat.
◆ Crush the remaining garlic cloves and mix with the breadcrumbs, warmed jelly, parsley and mustard, and season well with salt and pepper.
◆ Smear this mixture over the lamb racks and leave for 1 to 2 hours. Roast for 25 to 35 minutes, until well browned but still pink in the centre.

SHEPHERD'S BUSH CASSOULET

INGREDIENTS

SERVES 6—8

750 g/1 lb white haricot (navy) beans

225 g/½ lb piece raw, unsalted bacon

225 g/½ lb Toulouse or Polish sausage, cut into 2½ cm/1 in chunks

1 kg/2 lb boned shoulder or breast of lamb cut into 3½ cm/1½ in chunks

seasoned flour

45 ml/3 tbsp olive oil

2 medium onions, sliced

4 cloves of garlic, crushed

30 g/2 tbsp tomato purée (paste)

5 g/1 tsp sugar

2½ g/½ tsp dried thyme/a bayleaf

2½ g/½ tsp dried oregano

1¼ cups/275 ml/½ pt red wine

salt and pepper

2 cups/550 ml/¾ pt stock or water

oven temperatures
200°C/400°F/Gas 6 and
160°C/325°F/Gas 3

PREPARATION

This version of the celebrated French dish — on the precise recipe for which, incidentally, no two Frenchmen have been known to agree — evolved when I was living near Shepherd's Bush market in London.

♦ Wash the haricot (navy) beans and soak them in cold water overnight.

♦ Change the water, add the bacon and the bayleaf and simmer, covered, for an hour. Drain, discard the bayleaf and cut the bacon into 2½ cm/1 in chunks. Put the bacon, beans and Toulouse or Polish sausage into a large casserole.

♦ Roll the meat in seasoned flour and brown in oil. Transfer to the casserole.

♦ Fry the onions and garlic in the remains of the oil until they begin to brown. Add the tomato purée, sugar, herbs, wine and plenty of salt and pepper. Simmer for a couple of minutes, then pour into the casserole together with the stock or water.

♦ Put the casserole, uncovered, into a hot oven for 20 minutes, stirring gently from time to time. Cover the casserole, turn down the heat and cook for a further 2½ hours, stirring occasionally, until the lamb and beans are tender.

♦ You may need to add a little more water if it looks like getting dry.

♦ This keeps extremely well in the fridge—one Cassoulet used to last me a week!

PORK AND GARLIC SATAY

INGREDIENTS

SERVES 6

1 head of garlic, unpeeled (about 15 cloves)

2½ g/½ tsp ground cumin

5 g/1 tsp ground coriander

2½ g/½ tsp ground cinnamon

5 g/1 tsp turmeric

⅓ cup/75 g/3 oz sugar

⅓ cup/75 ml/3 fl oz lime juice

sprigs of lemon verbena or lemon balm, well bruised (optional)

4 scallions, chopped

30 ml/2 tbsp oil

1 kg/2 lb lean pork

a small Spanish onion, finely chopped

2½ cm/1 in root ginger, grated

chilli (chili) powder to taste

1½ cups/175 g/6 oz raw peanuts, roasted and ground

salt to taste

PREPARATION

♦ To make the marinade, peel and crush 3 of the garlic cloves and combine with the cumin, coriander, cinnamon, turmeric, 10 g/2 tsp of sugar, 2 tbsp/30 ml/1 fl oz of lime juice, the lemon verbena or lemon balm, the scallions and 15 ml/1 tbsp of oil.

♦ Put the cubed pork into a plastic bag and pour in the marinade. Tie up the top of the bag and put it on a plate in case it leaks, and leave in a cool place for 2 to 4 hours.

♦ Plunge the remaining unpeeled garlic cloves into boiling water and simmer for 10 minutes or until just tender. Drain, peel and cut each clove lengthwise into 3 or 4 pieces.

♦ To make the sauce, fry the onion in the remaining oil with the grated ginger and the chilli (chili) powder—don't put in too much—you can always add more later—until transparent.

♦ Drain the marinade from the pork, remove the lemon verbena or lemon balm, and add to the onion. Simmer for several minutes.

♦ Add the remaining lime juice, sugar, and the peanuts. Season with salt, extra chilli if necessary, and simmer until thickened.

♦ Thread the marinaded pork cubes and garlic slices alternately onto thin skewers—wooden ones are traditional—5 to 7 pork cubes to each, and either grill (broil) for about 10 minutes, turning once, or barbecue, basting with a little oil, until glistening brown and cooked.

LIVER STROGANOFF

INGREDIENTS

SERVES 4

450 g/1 lb calves' liver, thinly sliced

1 clove of garlic, crushed

15 ml/1 tbsp oil

2½ g/½ tsp fresh bruised sage leaves, chopped

6 black peppercorns, bruised

2½ g/½ tsp paprika

30 ml/2 tbsp dry white wine or dry sherry

approx 2 cups/225 g/½ lb baby onions

4 tbsp/50 g/2 oz butter

4 tbsp/25 g/1 oz flour

5 ml/1 tsp garlic juice

⅔ cup/150 ml/5 fl oz soured (sour) cream

salt and pepper

PREPARATION

◆ Cut the liver into strips ½ cm × 5 cm/¼ in × 2 in.

◆ Pour over them a mixture of the crushed garlic, oil, sage, peppercorns, paprika and wine or sherry, and leave to marinate in a cool place for 2 to 4 hours, stirring occasionally.

◆ Peel the onions—this is easier if you first loosen the skins by blanching them in boiling water for 30 seconds—and sweat them in the butter, covered, for 10 to 20 minutes, until they are just tender. Remove the onions from the pan and reserve.

◆ Drain the liver of its marinade, toss it in the flour and cook in the butter and onion juices for no more than a minute on each side.

◆ Add the garlic juice and onions, and simmer for a minute more.

◆ Off the heat, stir in the sour cream, season with salt and pepper to taste and serve immediately.

DOUBLE GARLIC CHICKEN

INGREDIENTS

SERVES 4—6

3 heads garlic (about 35 cloves)

1½-2 kg/3½-4 lb roasting chicken

¾ cup/175 g/6 oz cream cheese or low fat soft cheese

15 g/1 tbsp chives, chopped

15 g/1 tbsp parsley, chopped

salt and pepper

225 g/½ lb green grapes (seedless and not too sweet)

a sprig of rosemary

2 tbsp/30 g/1 oz butter

oven temperature
180°C/350°F/Gas 4

PREPARATION

◆ Plunge the unpeeled garlic, except for 2 cloves, into a pan of boiling water for 30 seconds, drain and peel.

◆ Boil for a further 2 minutes, drain and set to one side.

◆ Peel one of the remaining garlic cloves and cut it in half. Rub the cut side of the garlic over the breast and legs of the chicken, then slice it and its other half.

◆ Peel and crush the last garlic clove and blend it with the cream or low fat cheese, chives and parsley. Season well with salt and pepper.

◆ Work your fingers under the skin of the chicken breast, carefully freeing it from the meat without tearing it.

◆ Pack the cheese mixture between the loosened skin and the meat, covering the breast completely.

◆ Stuff the body of the chicken with the blanched garlic and the grapes, together with most of the rosemary.

◆ Put the chicken in an oiled roasting pan and tuck slices of garlic and the remaining blades of rosemary between the legs and wings and the body of the chicken.

◆ Sprinkle the breast with salt and dot it with the butter. Cover the breast and feet with foil.

◆ Bake for approximately an hour and a half, until the juice no longer runs pink, removing the foil for the last 20 minutes of cooking to crisp the skin.

CHICKEN CREOLE

INGREDIENTS

SERVES 6–8

8 chicken portions

¾ cup/100 g/4 oz peeled prawns (shrimp)

2 tbsp olive oil

2½ g/½ tsp dried tarragon

2 cloves of garlic, crushed

1¼ g/¼ tsp hot pepper sauce or cayenne

1 large onion, thinly sliced

1 red pepper, cored and thinly sliced

Concentrated Tomato Sauce (see page 59)

oven temperatures
180°C/350°F/Gas 4 and
220°C/425°F/Gas 7

PREPARATION

♦ Score the chicken pieces and put them in a dish, with the prawns (shrimp) at one end. Pour over them a mixture of the oil, tarragon, garlic and hot pepper sauce or cayenne. Leave to marinate for at least an hour before cooking.

♦ Drain the marinade into a frying pan and remove the prawns and keep to one side until needed.

♦ Fry the chicken in the heated marinade for 7 to 10 minutes, turning occasionally, until well browned. Arrange in a roasting pan.

♦ Fry the onion and sweet pepper in the oil left in the pan until the onion begins to brown, then arrange over the chicken.

♦ Pour the tomato sauce over the vegetables and chicken, cover the pan with foil, and cook at the lower temperature for 30 minutes.

♦ Remove the foil, turn up the heat and bake for another 20 minutes, adding the prawns 5 minutes before serving, to heat them through.

VARIATIONS

This is a good way of cooking cod steaks—there is no need to fry them first.

BOXING DAY MOLE

INGREDIENTS

SERVES 8

turkey bones

5 cups/1 1/2 pt water

2 medium onions, coarsely chopped

4 cloves of garlic, coarsely chopped

salt and pepper

⅔ cup/100 g/4 oz canned pimentos, coarsely chopped

1 small red pepper, seeded and chopped

¾ cup/225 g/½ lb ripe tomatoes, skinned, seeded and chopped

1 thick slice of white bread, toasted and crumbled

1 cup/100 g/4 oz ground almonds

⅓ cup/50 g/2 oz sesame seeds

30 ml/2 tbsp oil or lard

5 g/1 tsp ground coriander

2½ g/½ tsp ground allspice

chilli (chili) powder to taste

10 g/2 tsp brown sugar

¼ cup/50 g/2 oz unsweetened chocolate, in small pieces

1 kg/2 lb cold turkey meat, torn into bite-sized pieces

PREPARATION

This streamlined version of one of Mexico's most famous national dishes makes a change from the usual methods of dealing with the remains of the Christmas or Thanksgiving turkey, and is equally good made with chicken. Serve it with plain boiled rice, refried beans, tortillas, a bowl of Guacamole (see page 40) and lots of lager or beer.

♦ Gently simmer the turkey bones in the water with a third of the onion, a quarter of the garlic, and plenty of salt and pepper, for 45 minutes, by which time you should have a good stock.

♦ Combine the remaining onion and garlic, pimentos, red pepper, tomatoes, bread, ground almonds, half the sesame seeds and half the turkey stock, and reduce to a smooth purée.

♦ In a large, heavy saucepan, heat the oil or lard, coriander, allspice, chilli (chili) powder—you can always add more later if it's not hot enough for you—and brown sugar, for a couple of minutes.

♦ Add the puréed sauce and stir over a moderate heat for 5 minutes. Add the chocolate and enough stock to dilute the sauce to the thickness of double cream. Season with salt and pepper to taste.

♦ Turn down the heat and cook gently, stirring occasionally, for 10 minutes. Add the turkey and heat for a further 10 minutes.

♦ Toss the remaining sesame seeds over a moderate heat until toasted and sprinkle them over the turkey just before serving.

GAIL'S CHICKEN WINGS

INGREDIENTS

SERVES 3—4

2 cloves of garlic, crushed

45 ml/3 tbsp oil

3 pinches cayenne

2½ g/½ tsp oregano

5 g/1 tsp paprika

10 ml/2 tsp vinegar

5 g/1 tsp sugar

30 ml/2 tbsp white wine

salt and pepper

10 chicken wings

seasoned flour

PREPARATION

♦ Combine the garlic, half the oil, the cayenne, oregano, paprika, vinegar, sugar, white wine and plenty of salt and pepper.
♦ Cut a few slits in each chicken wing and put them in a large plastic bag.
♦ Pour over the marinade and knot the top of the bag. Put the bag in a bowl in case of leaks, and leave in a cool place for 2 to 4 hours.
♦ Drain the chicken wings of the marinade and toss them in the seasoned flour.
♦ Fry in the remaining oil for approximately 10 minutes, turning occasionally, until well browned.

———————————TO SERVE———————————

Drain on kitchen paper towels and serve hot with brown rice and salad.

COLD CHICKEN MILLEFOGLIE

INGREDIENTS

SERVES 4—6

350 g/³⁄₄ lb puff pastry

¹⁄₂ cup/100 ml/4 fl oz Basic Garlic Dressing (see page 58)

8—10 canned artichoke hearts, quartered

7 ml/¹⁄₂ tbsp oil

1 clove of garlic, crushed

5 g/1 tsp ground coriander

2¹⁄₂ g/¹⁄₂ tsp ground cumin

2¹⁄₂ g/¹⁄₂ tsp turmeric

2¹⁄₂ g/¹⁄₂ tsp paprika

2 pinches cayenne pepper

15 ml/1 tbsp lemon juice

1 cup/100 g/4 fl oz stiffly whipped cream

1¹⁄₃ cups/225 g/8 oz cold cooked chicken, cut or torn into bite-sized pieces

salt and pepper

30 g/2 tbsp finely chopped parsley

15 g/1 tbsp mayonnaise or Aïoli (see page 55)

oven temperature
230°C/450°F/Gas 8

PREPARATION

♦ Roll the pastry out thinly and cut into 3 strips approximately 10 cm/ 4 in wide. Prick all over with a fork and bake for 7 to 10 minutes until well-risen and browned. Cool on wire rack until needed.

♦ Warm the Basic Garlic Dressing and pour over the artichoke hearts. Set aside for at least 1 hour.

♦ To make the sauce for the chicken, heat the oil and add to it the garlic, coriander, cumin, turmeric, paprika, and cayenne. Stir over a moderate heat for several minutes. Remove from the heat and add the lemon juice, and either pour or strain the mixture into the cream. Fold the chicken into the sauce and season with salt and pepper to taste.

♦ To assemble the Millefoglie, put one slice of cooked pastry on a serving dish and spread over it half the chicken mixture. Drain the dressing from the artichoke hearts, mix into them the parsley and put half of this on top of the chicken. Top with the second piece of pastry, the remaining chicken, and the rest of the artichoke mixture.

♦ Spread the underside of the final pastry slice with the mayonnaise or Aïoli and press it gently, sticky side down, onto the artichoke and parsley mixture.

————————————TO SERVE————————————

Slice with a very sharp serrated knife and serve immediately.

SCALLOPED SWEET POTATOES

INGREDIENTS

SERVES 4–6

6 cups/675 g/1½ lb sweet potatoes

1 small onion, thinly sliced

2 cloves of garlic, finely chopped

2 tbsp/25 g/1 oz seasoned flour

⅔ cup/150 ml/¼ pt milk

2 tbsp/25 g/1 oz butter

10 g/2 tsp brown sugar (optional)

oven temperature
200°C/400°F/Gas 6

PREPARATION

This recipe is usually made with ordinary baking potatoes, but I find sweet potatoes and garlic an unusually good combination, especially served with fish or ham.

♦ Scrub the sweet potatoes and cut, unpeeled, into slices no more than ¼ cm/⅛ in thick.

♦ Line a well-greased baking dish or small roasting pan with a layer of potato slices and sprinkle with the sliced onion, garlic and seasoned flour.

♦ Repeat the layers, finishing with sweet potatoes.

♦ Pour in enough milk to come about half way up the potatoes, and dot with the butter.

♦ Sprinkle on the brown sugar, and bake for 30 to 45 minutes, depending on thickness.

BUTTER-BRAISED GARLIC

INGREDIENTS

SERVES 3–4

4 good-sized heads of garlic
(about 60 cloves)

6 tbsp/75 g/3 oz butter

salt and pepper

TO SERVE

30 g/2 tbsp fresh parsley, finely
chopped

PREPARATION

Garlic was popular as a vegetable during the Middle Ages and was known as "aquapatys". It is certainly time that this surprisingly subtle dish had a revival.

♦ Separate the garlic cloves and simmer in salted water for 15 minutes, until just tender.

♦ Drain, peel carefully and stew them in the butter over a low heat for a further 5 to 7 minutes. Season with salt and pepper.

————————TO SERVE————————

Stir in the chopped parsley and serve.

INTERALLIA

INGREDIENTS

SERVES 4–6

*3 heads unpeeled garlic
(about 35 cloves)*

2 cups/350 g/³⁄₄ lb baby onions

4 tbsp/50 g/2 oz butter

*approx 3 cups/350 g/³⁄₄ lb young
leeks, trimmed and cut into
2¹⁄₂ cm/1 in chunks*

¹⁄₂ cup/100 ml/4 fl oz water

2 tbsp/25 g/1 oz flour

2¹⁄₂ g/¹⁄₂ tsp English mustard

1¹⁄₄ g/¹⁄₄ tsp turmeric

2¹⁄₂ g/¹⁄₂ tsp sugar

²⁄₃ cup/150 ml/¹⁄₄ pt hot milk

*45 ml/3 tbsp single (light or cereal)
cream*

salt and pepper

TO SERVE

*15 g/1 tbsp finely chopped spring
onions or scallions (green part only)*

15 g/1 tbsp chives, finely chopped

PREPARATION

This dish is so named because it combines five of the allium *family in
one delicious vegetable mixture.*

♦ Separate the garlic cloves and blanch them together with the onions
in boiling water for a couple of minutes. Drain and peel.

♦ Cook them very gently in half the butter for 7 to 10 minutes, then
add the leeks and the water. Bring to the boil and set to one side.

♦ Melt the remaining butter in a small saucepan, add the flour,
mustard, turmeric and sugar, and stir for a few minutes.

♦ Turn up the heat, strain the liquid from the vegetables into it and
add the hot milk. Simmer for 5 minutes.

♦ Pour over the vegetables and continue to simmer until they are *just*
tender.

♦ Remove from the heat and gently stir in the cream, and season with
salt and pepper to taste.

―――――――――――――――――TO SERVE―――――――――――――――――

Sprinkle with the spring onions or scallions and the chives.

This dish is especially good with lamb or gammon (ham).

RATATOUILLE

INGREDIENTS

SERVES 6—8

2 large onions, coarsely chopped

3 cloves of garlic, crushed

60 ml/4 tbsp olive oil

2 medium-sized aubergines (eggplants), cut into chunks

3 large red peppers, seeded and sliced

2 medium courgettes (zucchini), cut into rings

2¼ cups/675 g/1½ lb ripe tomatoes, peeled and coarsely chopped

5 g/1 tsp sugar

salt and pepper

TO SERVE

30 g/2 tbsp parsley, chopped (optional)

PREPARATION

This French classic can be eaten either hot or cold; as a side dish, a topping for pasta or as a meal in itself with lots of grated cheese.

♦ Cook the onions and garlic in the oil over a low heat for approximately 15 minutes, until transparent.

♦ Add the aubergines (eggplants), peppers and courgettes (zucchini). Cover the pan and simmer for half an hour, or until the vegetables are just tender.

♦ Add the tomatoes, sugar and season to taste. Cook for a further five minutes.

———————TO SERVE———————

Sprinkle the parsley over the Ratatouille just before serving.

GLAZED GARLIC NEEPS

INGREDIENTS

SERVES 4

2 heads garlic (about 25 cloves), unpeeled

3½ cups/450 g/1 lb young turnips, quartered

⅔ cup/150 ml/¼ pt water

4 tbsp/50 g/2 oz butter

22 g/1½ tbsp sugar

salt and pepper

TO SERVE

15 g/1 tbsp parsley, finely chopped

PREPARATION

◆ Separate the garlic cloves and blanch them in boiling water for 5 minutes, drain and peel.

◆ Put the garlic, turnips, water, butter, sugar and a little salt and pepper into a heavy saucepan and cook gently in a covered pan for about 20 minutes, until the garlic and turnips are tender, but not mushy. If by then the liquid has not evaporated to a syrupy glaze, uncover the pan and quickly boil off the excess.

TO SERVE

Check the seasoning and serve, sprinkled with the parsley.

This is very good with most roast meats, particularly beef and ham.

GARLIC MASH

INGREDIENTS

SERVES 6

3 heads garlic (about 35 cloves)

½ cup/100 g/4 oz butter

2 tbsp/25 g/1 oz flour

1¼ g/¼ tsp nutmeg

1¼ g/¼ tsp English mustard

1¼ cups/275 ml/½ pt boiling milk

salt and pepper

8 cups/1 kg/2 lb floury potatoes

45 ml/3 tbsp single (light or cereal) cream

PREPARATION

♦ Separate the garlic cloves and blanch them in boiling water for 1 minute, drain and peel.

♦ Cook them over a low heat, covered, in half the butter for about 20 minutes until tender.

♦ Blend in the flour, nutmeg and mustard, and stir for several minutes without browning.

♦ Remove from the heat and stir in the boiling milk. Season with plenty of salt and pepper.

♦ Return to the heat and simmer for 5 minutes. Sieve or blend to a smooth purée.

♦ Return to the pan and simmer for 2 more minutes.

♦ Peel the potatoes and cut into small chunks. Boil for 15 minutes or until just tender and drain. Mash with the remaining butter.

♦ Beat in the reheated garlic purée followed by the cream, a spoonful at a time. The final mixture should not be too runny. Season with salt and pepper to taste and serve immediately.

Garlic Mash is particularly good with sausages, steak and roast chicken, or as a nest for baked eggs. Don't count on leftovers, but if there are any they can be chilled, shaped into patties, rolled in flour and shallow fried in hot fat until brown on both sides.

BONANZA BROWN RICE

INGREDIENTS

SERVES 4

2 cloves of garlic, crushed

1 medium onion, finely chopped

½ a small red pepper, thinly sliced

30 ml/2 tbsp oil

1 cup/225 g/8 oz brown rice

2 cups/450 ml/16 fl oz canned consommé

1 cup/225 ml/8 fl oz water

salt and pepper

PREPARATION

♦ Sauté the garlic, onion and sweet red pepper in the oil until the onion is transparent and beginning to brown.

♦ Add the rice and cook for several minutes, stirring well.

♦ Pour in the consommé and water, cover the pan and cook over a low heat for 30 to 35 minutes, until the rice is just tender. Season with salt and pepper and serve.

♦ This rice goes very well with chicken.

DAL

INGREDIENTS

SERVES 4

22 ml/1½ tbsp clarified butter or oil

3–4 cloves of garlic, crushed

10 g/2 tsp turmeric

1 small green chilli (chili), seeded and finely chopped or 2 pinches of chilli powder

10 g/2 tsp ground coriander

5 g/1 tsp ground cumin

2 medium onions, finely chopped

1 cup/200 g/7 oz red split lentils

3 cups/675 ml/1¼ pt water or stock

15 g/1 tbsp tomato purée (paste)

2½ g/½ tsp sugar

salt and pepper

PREPARATION

◆ Heat the clarified butter or oil in a large heavy pan and fry the garlic and spices for several minutes.
◆ Add the onion and when it begins to brown, add the lentils.
◆ Pour over the water or stock, add the tomato purée and sugar, and bring to the boil.
◆ Simmer the Dal for between 40 to 50 minutes, until the lentils begin to fall apart.
◆ Season with plenty of salt and a little pepper, and serve.

VARIATIONS

For a really tasty lentil soup, simply double the quantity of water or stock and either sieve or blend the cooked Dal.

Dal can also be made with yellow split peas, which must be soaked overnight in warm water. Cook the Dal for about an hour and a half, until the peas are tender.

Haricot (navy) bean salad

INGREDIENTS

SERVES 4

1 cup/225 g/½ lb dried white haricot (navy) beans

¾ cup/175 ml/6 fl oz Basic Garlic Dressing (see page 58)

2 cloves of garlic, crushed

1 large red pepper, seeded and thinly sliced

2 small leeks, thinly sliced

15 g/1 tbsp finely chopped spring onions or scallions (green part only)

PREPARATION

♦ Cover the beans with boiling water and leave to soak overnight.

♦ Pour off the soaking water. Cover with fresh water and boil for 1½ to 2 hours, until tender. You may need to add more water from time to time to prevent them sticking.

♦ Drain the beans and, while still hot, pour over the Basic Garlic Dressing. Stir in the crushed garlic and cool until needed.

♦ Before serving, stir in the pepper and leeks and sprinkle with the chopped spring onions or scallions.

VARIATIONS

Omit the leeks and spring onions or scallions, and stir in 30 g/2 tbsp of coarsely chopped fresh mint just before serving.

CHICORY ORANGE WALNUT SALAD

INGREDIENTS

SERVES 4—6

4 plump heads chicory (Belgian endive)

2 large sweet oranges

¾ cup/75 g/3 oz walnut halves

45 ml/3 tbsp olive or walnut oil

15 ml/1 tbsp lemon juice

1 clove of garlic, finely crushed

2½ g/½ tsp sugar

PREPARATION

♦ Cut the chicory into 1¼ cm/½ in slices.
♦ Peel and slice the oranges—or divide them into segments—removing the skin and pith from each.
♦ Coarsely chop the walnuts, reserving a few for decoration.
♦ Mix the olive or walnut oil, lemon juice and sugar, and pour this dressing over the combined chicory, orange and walnuts.
♦ Decorate with the reserved walnuts and serve chilled.

PASTA SALAD

INGREDIENTS

SERVES 4

2 cups/225 g/8 oz dry pasta: bows,
shells or spirals

7½ ml/½ tbsp oil

15 g/1 tbsp Garlic purée (see page
113) or 2 cloves of garlic, crushed

⅔ cup/150 ml/5 oz mayonnaise

15 ml/1 tbsp single (light or cereal)
cream

1¼ cups/175 g/6 oz button
mushrooms, quartered

1 cup/175 g/6 oz thinly sliced
French garlic sausage, cut into
strips and fried till crisp

25 g/1½ tbsp spring onions or
scallions, finely chopped

salt and pepper to taste

PREPARATION

♦ Cook the pasta with the oil in lots of salted boiling water for 15 to
20 minutes, until just tender. Drain well, and while still warm stir
in the remaining ingredients.
♦ Serve warm or chilled.

VARIATIONS

Vary the dressing by using half mayonnaise and half Pesto (see
page 54).
♦ Use Aïoli (see page 55) instead of the mayonnaise. You will
probably not need the extra garlic.
♦ Lots of other vegetables and nuts can be added, singly or in
combination: chopped or sliced sweet pepper, thinly sliced or
grated baby courgettes (zucchini), cubed avocado pear (avocado),
toasted peanuts, blanched almonds or walnuts, pine nuts.
♦ Pasta salad is also very good with ½ cup/100 ml/4 fl oz of Basic
Garlic Dressing (see page 58) instead of the mayonnaise and
cream. This dressing goes particularly well with quartered
artichoke hearts and browned cashew nuts.

TSATZIKI

INGREDIENTS

SERVES 4

1 large cucumber, unpeeled

2½ g/½ tsp salt

2 cloves of garlic, finely chopped

2 cups/450 g/¾ pt thick Greek yogurt

pepper

a little lemon juice

PREPARATION

◆ Coarsely grate the cucumber into a colander. Sprinkle with the salt and leave to drain for about 1 hour.

◆ Stir the drained cucumber and garlic into the yogurt and add pepper and lemon juice to taste.

◆ Serve chilled.

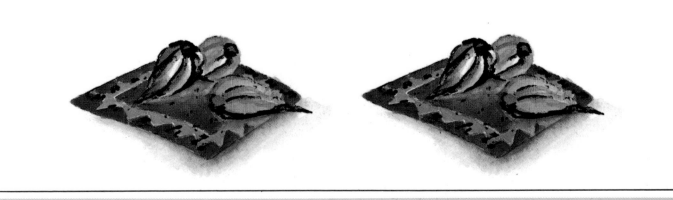

BREADS & PIZZA

Opposite: Garlic Bread (*see* page 104)

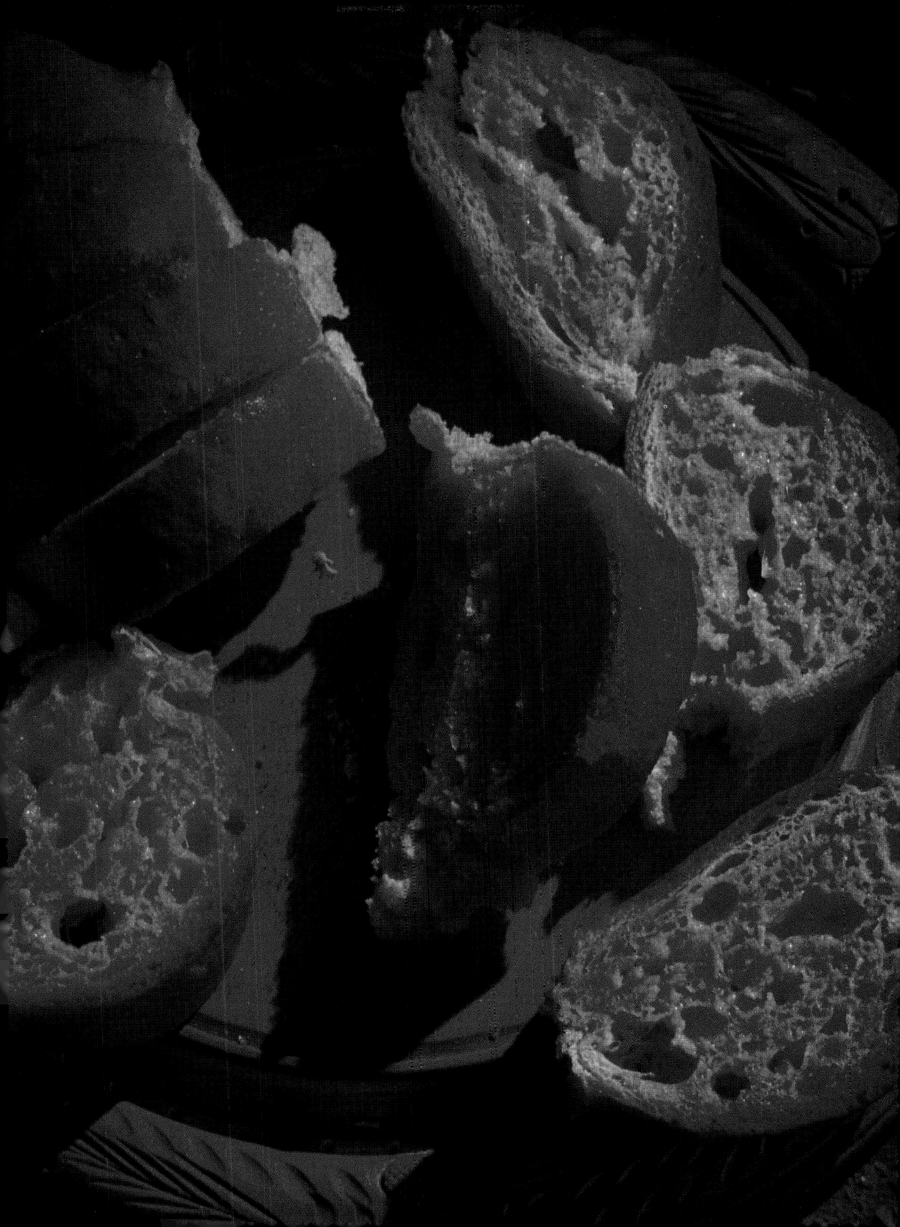

GARLIC BREAD

INGREDIENTS

1 French loaf

Garlic Butter (see page 60), softened

5 g/1 tsp mixed fresh herbs, chopped (optional)

oven temperature
180°C/350°F/Gas 4

PREPARATION

♦ Slice the bread, but not right through the bottom of the loaf.
♦ Spread both sides of each slice with the softened Garlic Butter and sprinkle with herbs.
♦ Wrap the loaf in foil and heat through in the oven for approximately 20 minutes.

—— VARIATIONS ——

Garlic Buns: Slice the top third off white or wholewheat buns and scoop out most of the crumb. Crumble this and toss it in melted Clarified Garlic Butter with some poppy seeds or mixed herbs. Pile the buttered crumbs into the bun shells, replace the tops and warm through before serving.

Garlic Pulled Bread: Scoop out the insides of a fresh white loaf with two forks in bite-sized pieces, stretching them slightly. Put them on a baking sheet and drizzle with melted Clarified Garlic Butter and bake at 190°C/375°F/Gas 5 until crisped.

Baked Garlic Croutons: Unlike fried garlic croutons, these can be kept warm in the oven until needed. Spread slices of white bread, crusts removed, with softened Garlic Butter. Cut into small cubes and arrange, butter side up, on a greased baking tray and bake at 190°C/375°F/Gas 5 until crisp and golden.

GARLIC MILK LOAF

INGREDIENTS

1 head garlic, about 12 cloves
1¼ cups/275 ml/½ pt milk
4½ cups/450 g/1 lb flour, warmed
5 g/1 tsp salt
2 tbsp/25 g/1 oz butter, melted
1 tbsp/15 g/½ oz fresh yeast
2½ g/½ tsp sugar
1 egg, well-beaten
rock salt
a little finely-chopped garlic (optional)
oven temperature 230°C/450°F/Gas 8

PREPARATION

◆ Blanch the separated, unpeeled, garlic cloves in boiling water for 5 minutes.

◆ Drain and peel them, and simmer in the milk for about 10 to 15 minutes, until tender.

◆ Sieve the flour with the salt and make a well in it.

◆ Either sieve or blend the milk and garlic until smooth, and add the melted butter.

◆ Cream the yeast with the sugar and add to the warm garlic milk with the beaten egg, and pour onto the flour.

◆ Mix the ingredients thoroughly and knead lightly until smooth. The dough should be soft.

◆ Leave to rise, covered, in a warm place for approximately 1 hour.

◆ Shape the dough into one large or two small loaves and place on a greased baking sheet. Cut several parallel slashes from end to end of each loaf, and leave to prove for 15 minutes.

◆ Sprinkle each loaf with rock salt and a little chopped garlic, and bake for 20 to 30 minutes until well browned and hollow-sounding when tapped underneath.

---VARIATIONS---

Leave the garlic cloves whole or add ⅓ cup/50 g/2 oz of pine nuts, browned in a little oil, to the dough before leaving to rise.

GARLIC SCONES

INGREDIENTS

MAKES 12

2¼ cups/225 g/8 oz flour

12½ g/2½ tsp baking powder

salt and white pepper

4 tbsp/50 g/2 oz butter or margarine

⅔ cup/150 ml/¼ pint milk and water, mixed

2 cloves of garlic, finely crushed

oven temperature
230°C/450°F/Gas 8

PREPARATION

♦ Sieve the dry ingredients together and rub in the butter or margarine until the mixture resembles fine breadcrumbs.
♦ Add the crushed garlic and enough of the milk to form a soft, but not wet, dough.
♦ Divide the dough in two, dust with flour and press each half into a round cake 2 cm/¾ in thick.
♦ Put each onto a baking sheet and divide into six with a knife, but do not separate the pieces.
♦ Bake for 10 to 15 minutes until the scones are brown and well risen, and the underside sounds hollow when tapped.
♦ Serve warm, split and buttered.

―――VARIATION―――

Add ⅓ cup/75 g/3 oz of coarsely chopped cheddar cheese to the dough before adding the milk and water.

PAN BAGNA

INGREDIENTS

SERVES 4

1 medium-sized white loaf
30 ml/2 tbsp olive oil
1 large onion, thinly sliced
2–3 cloves of garlic, finely chopped
1 cup/350 g/³⁄₄ lb tomatoes, skinned, seeded and sliced
12 stoned black olives
2½ g/½ tsp dried oregano
2½ g/½ tsp sugar
salt and pepper to taste

PREPARATION

◆ Slice off the top third of the loaf and scoop out most of the inside (this can be used as breadcrumbs in other recipes).

◆ Heat the oil and fry the onion and garlic until the onion begins to brown, turn down the heat and cook until the onions are transparent.

◆ Add the tomatoes, olives, oregano and sugar, and season with salt and plenty of freshly ground black pepper. Stir well and take off the heat.

◆ Fill the scooped-out loaf with this mixture (see the photograph) and put the top back on.

◆ Wrap the filled loaf in foil and enclose in a plastic bag. Weight it down with a plate and several cans.

◆ Leave in the fridge for 2 to 4 hours and serve cold in thick slices. This is superb picnic food.

―VARIATION―

Omit the onion and use 2 cups/700 g/1½ lb tomatoes. Mix together the tomatoes, garlic, oil, olives and sugar, and season well. Replace the dried oregano with 10 g/2 tsp of finely chopped fresh basil or marjoram.

PIZZA NAPOLITANA CON AGLIO

INGREDIENTS

SERVES 4

2¼ cups/225 g/½ lb flour, sifted

1 tbsp/15 g/½ oz fresh yeast

2½ g/½ tsp sugar

tepid water to mix

2½ g/½ tsp salt

2¼ cups/675 g/1½ lb ripe tomatoes, skinned, seeded and coarsely chopped

freshly ground black pepper

12 anchovy fillets

10 g/2 tsp finely chopped fresh basil

2–3 cloves garlic, finely chopped

1½ cups/175 g/6 oz mozzarella cheese, thinly sliced

22 ml/1½ tbsp olive oil

oven temperature
230°C/450°F/Gas 8

PREPARATION

♦ Put the flour into a large bowl and make a well in the middle.
♦ Mix the yeast, sugar and 30 ml/2 tbsp of the tepid water in a cup and pour into the flour.
♦ Add the salt and mix well, adding enough tepid water to make a stiff dough.
♦ Knead on a well-floured board until light and elastic. Cover with a clean towel and leave in a warm place for 2 to 2½ hours until doubled in size.
♦ Roll the dough into a circle ½ cm/¼ in thick, and put it onto a large, well-oiled baking sheet. Leave to prove for 10 minutes.
♦ Top with the tomatoes, plenty of pepper, garlic, and basil followed by the anchovies and sliced mozzarella cheese. Finally sprinkle oil over the top.
♦ Bake for 25 to 35 minutes, until the dough is cooked and the cheese bubbles.

HI-SPEED PIZZAS

INGREDIENTS

MAKES 4 SMALL PIZZAS

2¼ cups/225 g/½ lb flour

2½ g/½ tsp salt

5 g/1 tsp baking powder

60 ml/4 tbsp olive oil

water to mix

1 cup Concentrated Tomato Sauce
(see page 59)

5 g/1 tsp fresh marjoram or
2½ g/½ tsp dried oregano

⅓ cup/50 g/2 oz stoned black olives

1½ cups/175 g/6 oz cheddar cheese,
thinly sliced

1 clove of garlic, finely chopped

oven temperature
230°C/450°F/Gas 8

PREPARATION

♦ Sift together the flour, salt and baking powder, and add the oil and enough water to make a very sticky dough.
♦ Divide into 4 and press each piece into a well-oiled 15 cm/6 in round pizza or pie pan.
♦ Top each with the tomato sauce, marjoram or oregano, olives and cheese, and sprinkle with the garlic.
♦ Bake for 15 to 20 minutes until the dough is cooked and the cheese is browned and bubbling.

—VARIATION—

You can add chopped ham, crisp bacon, strips of salami, sliced button mushrooms or sliced red pepper.

PRESERVES

Opposite: Garlic Pepper Essence (*see* page 112)

GARLIC PEPPER ESSENCE

INGREDIENTS

10 garlic cloves

5 small chilli (chili) peppers

cooking sherry

PREPARATION

A few drops of this essence really perks up soups and stews, but because it is very intense, it should be used with caution.

♦ Peel and halve the garlic and prick the peppers all over.

♦ Mix them together and pack into a wine bottle.

♦ Cover with the sherry and fill the bottle leaving room for the cork.

♦ Cork the bottle securely and leave, undisturbed, for a couple of weeks.

♦ The sherry can be topped up from time to time.

GARLIC VINEGAR

INGREDIENTS

8–10 cloves garlic

a little coarse salt

2½ cups/550 ml/1 pt white wine or tarragon vinegar

PREPARATION

This vinegar is very handy for salad dressings and marinades for fish, chicken and seafood.

♦ Crush the garlic finely with the salt and put into a large, heat-proof jar.

♦ Bring the vinegar to the boil and pour over the garlic.

♦ Allow to cool and then cover. Leave to infuse for 2 to 3 weeks.

♦ Strain and bottle for use.

VARIATION

Red wine Garlic Vinegar, for use in strongly flavoured marinades like those for stewing beef, pot roasts and game, is made by saving red wine bottle ends and letting them "turn". Use 10 cloves of garlic to 2½ cups/550 ml/1 pt of liquid, and warm the vinegar until hand hot before pouring over the crushed garlic.

GARLIC PURÉE

INGREDIENTS

4 heads garlic (about 50 cloves)

30 ml/2 tbsp olive oil

salt and pepper

PREPARATION

This is a useful and tasty addition to soups, stews, sauces, salad dressings—especially bought or home-made mayonnaise—and as a relish with cold meat. The cooking takes away any acrid flavours and the purée is far less crude and bitter than the commercially-produced version. It is also delicious spread on toast under poached or scrambled eggs.

♦ Simmer the unpeeled garlic cloves in lightly salted water for about 20 to 25 minutes, until soft. Drain and cool.
♦ Peel the garlic cloves, cutting off the tough root end and any discoloured patches.
♦ Mash to a smooth, sticky paste with a fork.
♦ Stir in the oil, and season with salt and pepper to taste.
♦ Pack into a glass jar and cover securely.
♦ This purée will keep in the fridge for 4 or 5 days, and can be frozen in cubes, using an ice-cube tray reserved for this purpose.

GARLIC PEPPER JELLY

INGREDIENTS

1¾ kg/4 lb sour apples

2 heads garlic (about 25 cloves)

10 small chilli (chili) peppers

5 cups/1 l/2 pts water

preserving sugar

PREPARATION

◆ Cut the apples into 2½ cm/1 in chunks, but do not peel or core them.
◆ Separate and peel the garlic cloves and cut each in half lengthways. Halve the peppers.
◆ Put the apples, garlic and peppers into a preserving pan with the water and stew for about an hour, until the apples are reduced to pulp. Tip into a jelly bag, or thick cloth, and leave to drain overnight. Do not be tempted to speed up the flow of juice by squeezing the bag, as this will only make the juice cloudy.
◆ Measure the juice into a clean pan with 2 cups/450 g/1 lb of sugar for every 2½ cups/550 ml/1 pt of liquid. Stir over a gentle heat until the sugar has dissolved. Boil rapidly for 10 minutes, until a little of the jelly sets when cooled on a plate, and wrinkles when you push it with your finger.
◆ While the jelly is still hot, pour into dry, warmed jars, filling them almost to the brim. Cover the surface of the jelly with a disc of waxed paper. Put a cellophane or waxed paper cover over each jar, secure with thin string or a rubber band, and store in a dark, cool, dry place.
◆ This is a very good relish with roasts and cold meats.

GARLIC HONEY

INGREDIENTS

30 cloves of garlic, peeled

2 cups/675 g/1½ lb clear honey

PREPARATION

This is a useful addition to salad dressings and marinades, and for glazing pork and chicken before roasting. It is also a traditional remedy for coughs, cold sores and acne—and hard-core garlic fanciers have been known to pour it over ice cream!

♦ Put the garlic cloves in a large, screw-top jar and pour the honey over them. There should be about 2½ cm/1 in between the honey and the top of the jar.

♦ Cover the jar tightly and leave in a warm place for at least a week, turning upside down occasionally.

♦ The juices released by the garlic will begin to turn the honey syrupy, and the goodness—not to mention the flavour—of the garlic will pass to the honey.

DRINKS

Opposite: Margarita Mia (*see* page 118)

MARGARITA MIA

INGREDIENTS

SERVES 2

½ clove of garlic

salt

60 ml/4 tbsp tequila

22 ml/1½ tbsp fresh lime juice

10 ml/2 tsp Cointreau

crushed ice

PREPARATION

♦ Bruise the garlic and rub the cut side of the clove round the rims of two standard 90 ml/3½ oz cocktail glasses.
♦ Dip the rims of the glasses in salt and chill them.
♦ Shake the tequila, lime juice and Cointreau together with ice in a screw-top jar and strain—so that the ice doesn't dilute the drink—into the prepared glasses.

GARLIC VODKA

INGREDIENTS

¾ cup/75 g/3 oz cloves of garlic

2½ cups/550 ml/1 pt vodka

15 g/1 tbsp sugar

PREPARATION

♦ Blanch the unpeeled garlic cloves in boiling water for 30 seconds, drain and prick each clove several times.
♦ Put the garlic cloves into an empty wine bottle, add the sugar and pour over the vodka. Cork securely and leave for two to three months. Taste a little and, if not sufficiently garlicky, leave for longer.
♦ When the desired strength is reached, drain and rebottle. This will keep indefinitely.

──────────VARIATIONS──────────

Garlic Brandy can be made in the same way, but for Garlic Gin double the quantity of sugar.

A few strips of thinly peeled orange rind make a good addition.

LHASSI WITH A BANG

INGREDIENTS

SERVES 2

1¼ cups/275 ml/½ pt Greek yogurt

½ cup/100 ml/4 fl oz ice water

1 large clove of garlic, finely chopped

a pinch of salt

15 g/1 tbsp fresh mint, coarsely chopped

TO SERVE

sprigs of mint

PREPARATION

♦ Stir the ingredients together and serve in two chilled old-fashioned glasses, garnished with sprigs of mint.

GARLIC BLOODSHOT

INGREDIENTS

SERVES 4—6

¾ cup/175 ml/6 fl oz vodka

¾ cup/175 ml/6 fl oz chilled consommé or beef bouillon

1¼ cups/275 ml/10 fl oz chilled tomato juice

15 g/3 tsp garlic juice

5 g/1 tsp sugar

juice of half a lemon

5 ml/1 tsp Worcestershire sauce

salt and cayenne pepper to taste

PREPARATION

A cross between a Bloody Mary and a Bullshot; recommended for Sunday Brunch and/or hangovers.

♦ Stir the ingredients together in a glass jug, season with salt and cayenne pepper to taste, and serve over ice.

GARLIC MULL

INGREDIENTS

SERVES 4–6

1 bottle robust red wine

½ a lemon, thickly sliced

a small orange, stuck with 6 cloves

15 g/1 tbsp brown sugar

7½ cm/3 in piece of stick cinnamon, bruised

6 unpeeled cloves of garlic, bruised

a glass of port or brandy (optional)

TO SERVE

a little grated nutmeg

PREPARATION

This is marvellously warming on a chilly evening.

♦ Heat all the ingredients very slowly in a large, heavy saucepan to just below boiling point. Strain into mugs and top with a pinch of grated nutmeg.

...AND A FEW SURPRISES

Opposite: Green Fruit Salad (see page 124)

BOMBSHELL BROWNIES

INGREDIENTS

MAKES 12—15

3 cloves of garlic, finely chopped

½ cup/100 g/4 oz butter

1 cup/100 g/4 oz unsweetened cocoa

4 eggs, lightly beaten

1 cup/225 g/8 oz sugar (some of it brown, if you prefer)

1 cup/100 g/4 oz flour, sifted

¾ cup/100 g/4 oz walnuts, chopped

⅓ cup/50 g/2 oz blanched almonds

oven temperature
160°C/325°F/Gas 3

PREPARATION

Even without the garlic, these brownies will blow your socks off!

♦ Put the garlic and butter into a large bowl over a saucepan of water on a gentle heat.

♦ When the butter has melted, stir in the cocoa and mix well.

♦ Add the eggs, sugar, flour and walnuts, stirring well after each addition.

♦ Pour the mixture into a greased and floured 20 × 25 cm/8 × 10 in cake pan and decorate with the blanched almonds.

♦ Bake for approximately 35 minutes. The top should be springy, but the inside still slightly moist.

♦ Turn out onto a wire rack and cut into squares or bars.

LIME AND GARLIC GRANITA

INGREDIENTS

SERVES 6

2½ cups/550 ml/1 pt water

½ cup/100 g/4 oz sugar

3 cloves of garlic, quartered

1¼ cups/275 ml/½ pt freshly
squeezed lime juice

rind of a lime, finely grated
(optional)

TO SERVE

twists of lime peel

PREPARATION

♦ Boil the water, sugar and garlic together for 5 minutes. Strain and cool.
♦ Stir in the lime juice and grated lime peel, and freeze, stirring from time to time, until granular but still slightly mushy.

TO SERVE

Decorate with twists of lime peel and serve with thin shortbread or *langues de chat*.

On its own, this is refreshing between courses.

INDEX